CASH FLOW SURGE

101 No-Cost and Low-Cost Fast-Action Strategies

to

Boost Your Business Cash Flow

By

Alastair Thomson

CashFlowSurgeBook.com

Important note

This publication contains materials designed to assist readers in evaluating the merits of business ideas for education purposes only. However, there is no guarantee that every single strategy, or indeed any of them, will work in your exact situation. Your results depend on the effort you put in and a range of other factors outside the publisher's control, including market conditions, specific industry factors and the time available.

Nothing in this book should be construed as legal or financial advice and results are not guaranteed — your results may vary. Every business idea carries an inherent risk of failure so, while the publisher and author have made every attempt to verify the information provided in this book, no responsibility can be assumed for any error, inaccuracy, or omission.

The advice, examples and strategies contained in this book are not necessarily suitable for every situation. Evaluating business opportunities involves a range of complex legal and financial issues. You should always retain competent legal and financial professionals with expertise in your business and a current licence to operate in your jurisdiction to provide guidance in evaluating and pursuing a specific business idea.

Table of Contents

Introduction

In nearly 30 years as a Finance Director and CFO the number one problem I've seen every business owner struggle with is cash flow.

Running a business is hard. I've run businesses for myself and for other people, so I know first-hand just how hard it can be.

Ask business owners what troubles them and they'll often grumble about the people in their business not performing as well as they'd like, the customers who demand the earth without being prepared to pay a fair price for the services they receive, or the high taxes they pay even though billionaires seem to avoid paying any tax at all.

> **All those things trouble business owners. But they're not what keeps them awake at night.**

What keeps business owners awake at night is worrying about whether there's enough money coming in to meet this month's payroll, or to pay key suppliers for the materials they need to satisfy customer orders, or even being able to take enough cash out the business this month to pay their mortgage and feed their kids.

For a growing business, cash flow is even more of an issue – time and again business owners tie themselves in knots and risk their own personal assets to secure the funding their business needs.

> **As the old saying goes, often there's too much month left at the end of the money.**

Not so long ago the business world was very different. Competent, hard-working business owners didn't have nearly as much to worry about. With a sensible strategy in place, a solid business model and good people on the team, things tended to work out just fine.

But think about it - when did we last experience "the good times" ...when the money was good, and the living was easy?

In the last 20 years or so, the business world has become increasingly precarious.

Huge swathes of manufacturing industry have disappeared to low-cost producers in the Far East, undercutting home-grown businesses and devastating once-prosperous towns and cities across the country.

The rise of the internet means price-shopping has never been easier. Now even local bricks-and-mortar businesses are expected to provide the same — or better — prices than internet giants like Amazon despite having much higher overheads and paying a lot more tax.

Regulation, government interference, soaring taxes and sky-high business rates means every business owner works more hours than ever. Yet it's never been harder to run a profitable business. Sales are under pressure, costs are up, margins are squeezed, and customers take longer to pay.

No wonder business owners lose sleep over their cash flow.

But there is another way — I've spent my career helping businesses grow rapidly without needing to raid their cash reserves, plunder the owner's life savings or go cap in hand to the bank for a loan.

Now, for the first time, I've collected 101 of the best strategies I've either used myself or seen other people use successfully.

Each of the strategies you'll discover in *Cash Flow Surge: 101 No-Cost and Low-Cost Fast-Action Strategies to Boost Your Business Cash Flow* revitalises your cash flow, more or less instantly, and they're either completely free to implement or require an outlay of just pennies on the dollar.

They won't take up much of your time either. You can implement many of the *Cash Flow Surge* strategies in as little as a few minutes…a couple of hours at most… and some can even be delegated to one of your team.

What's more, these strategies have been selected because they pay off fast…in days or weeks, not months or years…boosting your profits and building your cash flow.

There's no need to read this book from front to back like a novel. The strategies don't build on the ones before, so can mostly be read in any order.

Simply pick one of the 101 no-cost and low-cost strategies in *Cash Flow Surge* and follow the easy action steps. When the first strategy is in play, pick another…then another…then another…

> **Layering a series of new cash-generating strategies, one on top of the other, means you multiply the cash flowing into your business, compounding the benefits and building up your cash flow faster than you might have thought possible.**

And all without having to invest heavily in new products and services…

Or needing armies of expensive consultants on eye-watering day rates to tell you what to do…

Or spend a fortune on the latest IT systems which claim to solve your every problem…but rarely do…

Or shelling out on expensive new machinery for the factory…

Or taking the chance that some magic "change programme" or "efficiency drive" will get you where you want to be…with McKinsey & Co research showing 70% of change programmes never achieve their objectives, the odds are very much against a change programme delivering the benefits you hoped it would.

In ***Cash Flow Surge*** we take the opposite approach. The 101 no-cost and low-cost strategies you'll discover in this book have been specially chosen because they're low-risk and easy to implement.

> **No specialist expertise required, no complicated processes to follow or obscure technical language to learn. And there's no big up-front cash investment to make or big demands on your time either.**

With zero cost up-front...or at worst a very modest investment with a rapid return...you can implement all 101 strategies in ***Cash Flow Surge*** without worrying about the cost.

You can try them all, one after another. And if, for whatever reason, one or two strategies aren't quite right for your industry or your business model, you've lost nothing.

But you've still got unlimited upside because every strategy that works releases a fresh surge of cash into your business that will pump away "hands-free" for years to come without any extra effort on your part.

And let's face it, a "next-to-no downside and unlimited upside" deal is hard to find these days.

So, if you're tired of worrying about your business cash flow and want to spend more time enjoying the fruits of your labour without worrying about how you're going to meet this month's payroll or next month's mortgage payment, ***Cash Flow Surge*** is for you.

> **These 101 no-cost and low-cost strategies take as little as a few minutes to implement...a couple of hours at most. They require no specialist knowledge or expert qualifications. Any business owner can put them into practice in minutes.**

And the strategies in ***Cash Flow Surge*** pay off fast, often in as little as a week or two.

Implement even a fraction of the ideas in this book and you'll generate fresh sources of cash flow for your business which means you won't be worrying about cash like you used to.

That takes away a lot of the stress of running your business. And you'll be able to capitalise on fresh business opportunities that come your way without worrying about whether you can afford to get involved.

You can spend your time doing what you want with your business and rediscovering the passion that led you to set up your business in the first place, instead of doing whatever you have to do to make sure there's enough cash in the bank to make this month's payroll.

In short, you spend less time trying to balance your chequebook and more time building your business. You're beholden to no-one.

As a business owner, that's where you want to be.

Let's get you there as fast as we can.

Alastair Thomson
Finance Director and CFO
CashFlowSurgeBook.com

About the Author

Alastair Thomson specialises in helping businesses increase revenues, reduce costs and build stronger cash flow. A Law graduate and qualified accountant he's spent the last 30 years helping entrepreneurs and household name brands build great businesses across the manufacturing, marketing, higher education, business services and professional services sectors.

In addition to his experience as a Finance Director and CFO, Alastair is an experienced Chairman, Chief Executive and Non-Executive Director, with a background in leading commercial and business development for businesses of all sizes.

Strategy 1 – Job done...what next?

If your business is like most others, it's not until the end of the month that invoices are raised for all the work done during the month.

Nobody likes doing paperwork so whether it's you, your office manager or your accounts clerk in charge of this task, sending out an invoice is rarely anyone's priority.

At least until the last day of the month when everyone knows they're supposed to get the bills out, and there's a flurry of last-minute invoice typing.

There are lots of reasons why this isn't a great strategy.

Firstly, it means very little else gets done on "invoicing day". People know they're up against the clock, so the phones go unanswered and the customer queries get ignored. No interruptions of any kind are tolerated on invoicing day.

Secondly, it's easy to miss things when you're in a rush. Even if it's just something relatively minor like forgetting to add the special delivery charge you'd agreed with your customer earlier in the month at the time the work was done. That can easily slip someone's mind in the mad panic of "invoicing day".

It could even be forgetting to invoice a job altogether — I've seen that before, more often than you might imagine.

Perhaps the paperwork is misfiled, or lost, and a bill never gets raised at all. By the end of the month nobody can remember what they got up to in the first week of the month anyway. A lot has happened since then.

And thirdly, you're missing out on cash that could have been in your bank account instead of your customer's bank account. If customers pay on standard 30-day terms and you wait until the end of the month to raise your invoices, you've essentially given 60 days free credit to everyone you did something for on the first of the month, not the 30 days you agreed when you did the deal in the first place.

If you raise an invoice the day your job is finished, or at the latest the following day, you'll never forget to bill anything, and you'll always remember any extras you agreed with your customer at the time.

And you'll accelerate your cash flow by as much as 30 days, depending on your credit terms with your customers.

If you want to operate with positive cash flow, one of the best things you can do is make sure you bill every job as soon as it's completed.

This simple daily discipline makes all the difference to your bank account over the course of a month and makes sure you get the cash in from your customers before you have to pay it out to your suppliers. That way you never need to dip into your own cash reserves in order to fund a payment to your suppliers, keeping the cash flow in your business positive.

That's why speed is one of the key components of our Cash Flow Mastery system (details of this at the end of the book). Once you've re-aligned your business to generate more cash flow, the defining factor is how quickly you make it all happen. More on this later in the book.

Time investment: Nothing — it takes no longer to type up an invoice on the day you do the work than it does if you type it up at the end of the month.

Cash investment: Zero — this is a task you're doing anyway and already paying for. But doing it sooner means you get paid sooner, improving your cash flow and boosting your bank account up to 30 days faster.

Strategy 2 – Do the easy stuff before the hard stuff

Some substantial costs are pretty quick, simple and easy to check. So why not start there?

Insurance, broadband, telephony costs, internet hosting, utility bills and many similar services, in the UK at least, are easy to check using a price comparison website like moneysupermarket.com, comparethemarket.com and moneysavingexpert.com. If you're outside the UK, similar internet-based services exist in many other jurisdictions too.

Don't forget there's sometimes a cost-effective provider who isn't on one of those comparison sites. But equally, don't worry about chasing down every available option as that's unlikely to be a good use of your time.

If I'm looking for an insurance quote, for example, I go to one of the comparison sites — it doesn't really matter which one — and run my details through that. They come back with plenty of alternatives which match your existing cover to consider.

Then I always go to a non-comparison site source, just in case. Direct Line is my favourite, although there are others. Sometimes they're cheaper, sometimes they're not. But now you've got a raft of comparison site quotes and one from outside the ecosystem of whichever comparison site you chose to make sure their prices are reasonable.

Often, you'll be able to save substantial amounts of money, all of which stays in your bank account rather than going to your current suppliers at higher prices. And nowadays doing the switch via any comparison site is simple and easy. Pretty much everything is taken care of for you.

At a few minutes each for every service you compare this way...telephony, broadband, internet hosting and so on...there's really no downside and potentially a substantial upside if you save money on the bills you pay out every month.

Similarly, if you're a member of a business body like the Chamber of Commerce or the FSB, they often have bulk deals with a local supplier for common business essentials. They're always worth checking out too as you can save some cash and support your local economy at the same time.

Every penny you save means more money in your pocket, cutting your overdraft and boosting your pot for future investments.

Time investment: 10-15 minutes to price-check each service.

Cash investment: Zero — you only switch if there's a cash benefit to you.

Strategy 3 – They charged *HOW* much?

For the bigger bills you receive, how often do you check the prices?

Don't start checking every bill in your business personally because you'll do nothing else all month. But big bills are worth checking to make sure they're right.

When I ran a business in the printing industry, for example, we had three major costs – wages, paper and ink.

Wages were whatever people's contracts said, and I knew the payroll department was more than capable of getting that right, so I didn't spend too much time on that.

But it was worth my time to check at least a sample of the prices on the 3 or 4 paper deliveries we got each day and the ink delivery we had a couple of times a week. Together those costs were 50% of the price we charged to our clients and ran to millions of pounds a year.

Bear in mind these materials were sent in by the truckload, so the invoice for each delivery was several thousand pounds a time.

It might have taken me a couple of minutes per invoice to check the prices against what we'd agreed with our suppliers, but it meant that, after adding in the wages, I could be pretty certain that around 80% of our cost base was spot on to the penny every month.

That gave me a solid foundation to assess the business performance and, perhaps just as important, stopped me worrying that I might have missed something in the costs when we had a month that wasn't as good as we'd expected.

I knew that whatever else might have gone awry, our costs were absolutely nailed down so the problem must be elsewhere in the business. This saved a huge amount of time going back through weeks or months of invoices and accelerated tracking down the real source of any problems. This approach also gave me great peace of mind into the bargain.

The "big costs" in your business probably aren't ink and paper, but you'll have something similar – the costs which, including wages and salaries, will represent 70-90% of your business cost base. Make sure they're right, because even small slippages can eat into your cash flow and put your business under pressure.

While I didn't often find something, the occasional "unfortunate misunderstanding", as our suppliers usually called them, did creep into our invoices from time to time. So when I picked one of those up, it was worth thousands of pounds to the business in return for a couple of minutes' work.

In our case, if the bill for paper had been out by just 5% across the year...a fairly minor discrepancy you might think...that would have equated to an extra cost of £250,000 for us, in a business that was making £1m in profit at the time.

A difference as small as 5% in a business with tight margins can move bottom line profit up or down by a quarter, so it's worth keeping a keen eye on your big purchases.

Even an occasional query to your suppliers...and even if they do turn out to be a genuine "unfortunate misunderstanding"...it shows your suppliers you're paying attention to what they charge which minimises the chances they'll try it on when it comes to your business in the future.

It's well worth your time to check.

This strategy is a great example of another of the key elements of our Cash Flow Mastery programme – prioritisation. Concentrating most of your energy on what really matters means you generate ideas faster, blast through problems quicker and find solutions before your competition does. Details on this programme can be found towards the end of this book.

Time investment: A few minutes every now and again to check a few invoices for your major purchases — you don't need to check them all, a sample is fine.

Cash investment: Zero.

Strategy 4 – Extra, extra! Read all about it!

If you're checking the "big costs" personally, make sure someone in your accounts team is checking the other stuff in the same way.

For smaller items, I find that usually the price isn't the issue, it's the extras which suppliers try to slip in, hoping nobody notices. The £25 delivery charge they didn't tell you about, the surcharge for next day delivery, the additional charge for working their people overtime to get the job done, and so on.

If you're a supplier, and you put your mind to it - admittedly some sectors are notorious for this sort of practice — there are dozens of ways to slip in extra charges here and there if you're so minded.

If you're especially cynical, you might even expect most of those extras to be challenged, but even if only a handful get through, the supplier might rationalise to themselves, that's still "free money" for them.

Don't get caught out. Your firm should issue a purchase order for everything it buys and send it, normally by email to save cost, to your supplier. All purchase orders should state clearly on the front that no charges will be accepted for anything not listed on the purchase order without written authorisation from your company.

It's not that some suppliers won't try this on from time to time, but if you've got systems in place, especially the statement on the face of the purchase orders, that gives you maximum power in any negotiations and you'll catch out the more fly-by-night suppliers who try it on.

When your accounts team find that sort of thing, they should send a quick standard email to the supplier saying that their invoice is incorrect and won't be paid until it agrees with the purchase order, unless they have written authorisation for any extra costs in which case they should forward that to your accounts team.

That way, in the short term, that cash stays in your bank account rather than your suppliers, easing the pressure on your cash flow. And you'll almost certainly save some money each month by making sure every invoice received represents the costs you thought you were incurring...and not a penny more.

Time investment: An hour or two to set the system up with your accounts team, but there's no ongoing extra work for you, and minimal extra work for your accounts team because all they have to do is send a pre-prepared email to suppliers if an invoice doesn't match the purchase order.

Cash investment: Zero.

Strategy 5 – Cut out the half that doesn't work

American department store magnate, John Wanamaker, once said "Half the money I spend on advertising is wasted. Trouble is, I don't know which half".

In your marketing and advertising at the moment, the likelihood is that you're spending some money you don't have to — at least in the short term.

In the long term, there are plenty of good reasons to invest in building a brand. It will make your business more valuable and attracting new customers will be easier and quicker.

But most people looking for a cash flow surge in their business need an immediate injection of cash or they won't be around long enough to worry about their long-term business valuation. You can come back to building a brand. This is about survival in the short term.

So look at every ad your business ran in the last couple of months — online and offline — and ask yourself: "did this advertisement directly contribute towards making a sale?".

You need to be careful not to be dragged into thinking about it being good for your business image, good for your personal profile or having some other vague general benefit, such as a nice shot of your products.

The question is simple - did that particular ad lead directly to a sale?

If it didn't, stop running that ad and save the cash. Either put the money in the bank to pay down your overdraft or reinvest it in the ads which generate a return so you can run those ads more often, in more places.

Either is good — that way you generate more income, make more profits and build up your cash reserves.

Make sure you know how every ad performs. Be strict about the criteria. And stop running ads that don't lead directly to a sale until you've got cash in the bank. Then focus on building your brand — done well, this really is the best strategy for long-term business success...but only when you have the cash.

If cash is tight that sort of investment won't pay off fast enough, so you're usually better to prioritise areas where the return is more immediate and return to brand building later.

As we cover in the Cash Flow Mastery programme, knowing what levers you're pulling, and the results you expect to get, is critical to getting on top of your cash flow. More on this later.

Time investment: A couple of minutes per ad.

Cash investment: Zero.

Strategy 6 – It's not about the price — it's about the terms

Understandably, many business owners want to buy at the cheapest price. But sometimes suppliers take advantage of that and give a lower price in return for longer-term contracts.

It sounds good now, but would that deal still sound as good in 2 years' time as it does today? Perhaps not.

So take a look at your major supply contracts. Do you know when your commitment to purchase from that supplier ends?

Also check what notice period you have — some long-term contracts don't just run out, you need to give, say, three months' notice before the end of the contract period if you want to terminate it, otherwise the contract automatically renews for another year or two, locking in the rates you're paying now even if they're uncompetitive.

That matters because it means you're not just stuck with uncompetitive pricing now, you're stuck with it for several more years when you could have been saving money instead.

What looked like an attractive up-front price might become a millstone around your business in the years to come.

So go through your contracts and pull together a spreadsheet or put the contract end-dates in your calendar. Check the notice terms, if any, and put another note in your calendar a few weeks ahead of time to compare other providers and see if you can get a better deal.

Be careful though — you're not necessarily looking for the cheapest price. You don't want to overpay, but I always advise clients to willingly pay an extra percent or two in return for short-term contracts which allow you to get out quickly and renegotiate regularly.

In the long run that's likely to make sure you always get the best deal in the current market. And it stops you having the pressure of paying out on a long-term deal when the market has moved in the other direction.

And if a supplier is tempting you with a "special price" in return for a long-term deal, remember that sort of deal only makes economic sense to your supplier if they know the price is about to fall.

They're trying to lock in their profits. They're not trying to reduce their costs.

Don't let them play this game. Avoid long-term contracts wherever possible, even if it costs you slightly more. The flexibility you get to switch suppliers and being able to renegotiate prices regularly is well worth any "extra costs" in the short-term.

Remember, suppliers always get those savings back in the long term — and why wouldn't they as soon as you're a captive customer on a long-term contract?

Time investment: An hour or two to identify major supply contracts and diarise their end-dates so you're ready to switch and save money as quickly as possible.

Cash investment: There might be a modest short-term uplift in costs, but over the life of a contract you can save fortunes if you're not tied into an expensive, long-term contract you can't get out of.

Strategy 7 – Getting paid for stuff you've already done

Governments around the world spend a lot of taxpayer's money trying to incentivise business owners to do all sorts of things. You need to take maximum advantage of schemes which could put some extra cash in your pocket.

For example, in the UK at the moment there's a very favourable tax treatment for research and development costs.

And before you think "we don't do any R&D", think again.

HMRC define R&D as "…researching or developing a new process, product or service. Or improving on an existing one."

That's clearly quite a wide definition, and clearly there are some subtleties we don't have the space to go into here.

But most businesses naturally spend quite a lot of time trying to improve existing processes, products or services. So a lot more businesses are eligible to claim R&D Tax Credits than might immediately think they can. It's no longer just the reserve of people in white coats in a lab with microscopes and test tubes.

Plenty of businesses qualify, even if they don't see themselves as "doing research and development". And with the chunky tax savings on offer, it's a way to get a substantial windfall cash inflow into your business straight from the government.

Talk of tax credits and HMRC technicalities can sound a little off-putting at first. But the great news is you don't need to become an expert in obscure areas of tax law. A number of companies will review your business for free, or for just a nominal up-front cost to cover expenses, and only charge their full fee if they manage to claim money back on your tax bill for you.

That's a great deal for you — if they don't find anything, it costs you nothing, but if they find something you can claim, HMRC lets you reduce your taxable profits **by more than the costs you've already incurred**.

That means your business pays out less in Corporation Tax and you keep the cash instead of giving it to the government.

And if you're not making a profit at the moment, the government will even make a cash payment into your business instead of reducing your Corporation Tax bill, providing a positive boost to your cash flow when you need it the most.

Your external accountants might be able to help, although they tend to want to charge a fee and are less keen on the "payment by results" model. However, it's worth asking the question.

There are also a variety of specialist providers — check Google for some names as this is an ever-changing area of tax or ask your local Chamber of Commerce or trade body for some suggestions.

Any way of saving money that doesn't cost you anything unless it saves you more than you're spending has to be worth exploring.

Even more so when the cash comes from the government — it's like a refund on the high taxes you already pay as a business owner, so why shouldn't you get back as much as you can?

Time investment: A couple of hours to brief your accountant or specialist advisor — after that they'll do all the work.

Cash investment: Zero.

Strategy 8 – Keeping the lid on professional advisors

Your business needs good professional advisors. You can always get your tax return done for £50 by a non-qualified accountant working out of an office under the railway arches. But I don't recommend it — the tax authorities are likely to be pursuing you for all sorts of misdemeanours down the line because, frankly, £50 isn't enough to do a proper job.

Most professional advisors charge fees based on hourly rates which are broadly similar to one another at each level of the organisation (partner rates, senior associate rates, associate rates and so on). I equally don't recommend selecting a professional advisor based purely on their charge-out rates.

However, I do speak to clients regularly who get bills they weren't expecting from their professional advisors. Out of nowhere an employment dispute is settled and the lawyer sends in a bill for £20,000. In your mind, you were perhaps expecting £5,000, but because you don't deal with employment disputes every day of the week (and if you do, there's probably something far wrong in your business) you've no idea what the cost might be.

Or it's the end of the tax year and your accountant tots up all the time they've spent with you this year, multiplies it up by their hourly rate and sends a bill your way.

Here's what I recommend instead.

Agree a retainer with your key professional advisors so you know exactly what's going out your bank account every month. And agree what they will do in return.

An accountant might prepare your annual accounts and corporate tax return, for example, for a fixed annual fee which they divide into 12 and collect on a monthly basis via standing order.

Your lawyer might agree to give legal advice for a fixed monthly fee covering all the routine advice you'll need, even though they'll probably quote separately for any court actions or employment disputes because, in fairness, they're a much more bespoke piece of work.

You swap an unpredictable cost that, by the law of averages, usually comes in when you're least able to pay for it with a stable monthly cost you can budget for.

You'll probably get a better deal from your professional advisors too as they won't be looking to charge you for every time they pick up the phone or answer an email. They just take those costs as part of your overall fees. Across the year, those 6-minute segments can mount up to a tidy sum.

And your professional advisors have a guaranteed revenue stream now, so you'll get a deal on the fees too.

You might be surprised how much your professional advisors would prefer a steady monthly payment into their bank account, just like you would. So, it's always worth asking the question.

Time investment: A quick chat with each professional advisor to talk about how a retainer system might work, in their interests and yours, and agree a fee. The answer should be no more than you currently pay in total and ideally a little less to reflect the fact that you're giving them guaranteed monthly cash flow, making their business easier to run.

Cash investment: Zero. At the very least you won't receive another unexpected bill — more likely you'll save on the hourly rate and get a better service from being seen as a loyal client.

Strategy 9 – What's sauce for the goose...

What's sauce for the goose is sauce for the gander.

Once you've sorted out a monthly retainer for your professional advisors, why don't you offer a monthly retainer deal to your clients?

It won't work for every product or service, but the world is moving to a subscription economy for all sorts of things — newspapers, restaurant meals, hairdressers, maintenance engineers and many more.

There's a lot to like about subscriptions because you're guaranteed to get your cash. It turns up in your bank account on the first of every month on autopilot, and you don't need to spend any time and effort raising invoices, chasing payments and the like.

Not only that, you know the income is secure for the length of your deal — you might require 90 days' notice to terminate, for example, giving you time to find another customer if a current one decides to stop paying for your services in this way.

Furthermore, because subscriptions are paid in advance, you don't need to wait 30, 60 or 90 days to be paid. That alone does wonders for your cash flow even if you change nothing else in your business.

There are two key things to watch out for.

Firstly, make sure you price your services properly. You'll be stuck with those prices for quite some time, so make sure you're happy to live up to them and seek professional advice to set them at an appropriate level, if necessary.

Secondly, customer payments must be automatic — direct debit, standing order through the bank, regular charge to your customer's credit card, etc. If you have to raise an invoice which goes into a 30, 60 or 90-day payment cycle, the advantages of going to a monthly subscription model diminish considerably.

But as long as you get those aspects right, press ahead.

An old client of mine ran his computer support business by having all his customers on a monthly retainer scheme, which covered all his costs and his own drawings from the business. Then when special one-off projects not covered by the maintenance package came along, as two or three did every month, that gave him extra profits which he reinvested or took as a personal bonus at the end of the year. His hassle-factor in collecting the cash that kept his business afloat every month – virtually zero.

Why not try it out? You don't need to switch all your customers to this model. Pick one you think will be most receptive or just try it out with the next new customer who comes along, so you'll have no downside to giving the idea a spin.

If it works, just roll it out from there across the rest of your customer base when you're ready.

Not all customers will want to operate a retainer model, but those who do will make a big difference to your monthly cash flow. Guaranteed, hassle-free cash turning up in your bank account on a monthly basis, regular as clockwork, eliminates most of the hassles of running a business and allows you to concentrate on your own areas of skill and expertise instead of having to chase around for cash to meet this monthly payroll or keep the bank manager happy.

Time investment: An hour or two to double-check your pricing and make an offer to at least one customer. Then, when you're happy, rinse and repeat.

Cash investment: Zero.

Strategy 10 – Performance guaranteed

One of the fastest ways to give a positive injection of cash into your business is offering extended guarantees to your customers. This strategy is part of the pricing section of our Cash Flow Mastery programme — how you can charge as much as possible for what you do, whilst still offering good value to your customers.

When you structure extended guarantees right, they cost very little to deliver, but give your customers valuable piece of mind.

Just before I sat down to write this chapter, I opened a letter from the company I bought my teenage son's laptop from last year. We got a budget laptop for his schoolwork costing around £400 as we didn't want to be too much out of pocket if he dropped it or left it on the school bus (if you know anything about teenage boys, you'll recognise this was a wise precaution).

Now the initial 12-month guarantee is up, the people who sold the laptop to us are trying to persuade me to take out an extended maintenance plan at £104 for the first year, and an unspecified — but presumably higher — rate in subsequent years. For that, they'll fix the laptop if it broke, but if they couldn't fix it, they'd replace it with a new one.

Sounds like a great offer — let's do the maths.

I don't have any personal knowledge of this company's pricing and operations, but I'd guess the likelihood of a laptop from a major brand going wrong in the next 12 months is certainly under 10%...perhaps under 5%.

Whether or not you think that's a deal worth taking depends on your view of risk. You might do it for a mission-critical piece of equipment. You might not do it for the 5th laptop that lives in your house when there's another four to use if that one goes wrong.

Think about your business. What are you doing for your customers that you could offer an extended guarantee at the end of your initial guarantee period?

Risk averse customers, and those for whom you supply a mission-critical service, will be highly motivated to say "yes". And as long as you price it right, you'll build up a great income stream that costs you very little.

Going back to our laptop, from time to time will the laptop company have to give out a brand, new laptop out to someone when they can't fix one of their laptops? Yes, of course. But they've priced their extended guarantee to make sure they're still in the money.

After all, the laptop they sold me for £400 probably only cost them half that amount in the first place. And I guess a lot of the time, they pick up 3-4 years at £104 per year extra. So they spend £200 to get perhaps £400 in profit back again...not a bad deal however you look at it.

Which part of your product or service could you offer an extended guarantee for? There's usually something.

Set it up to collect monthly by some automated payment service like direct debit or regular credit card charge and it's more regular guaranteed cash flowing into your business for little or no extra cost to you.

Time investment: 1 hour to work out the pricing, then just get your sales team to offer the extended guarantee with every sale up front. For customers who say "no" (as I did in the shop originally) just diarise for 4-6 weeks before your standard guarantee expires and offer the same deal again.

Cash investment: The cost of a letter or a quick email to your customers...perhaps a pound or two per customer at most. For every customer who says yet, that's guaranteed extra cash flowing into your business in return for little or no outlay on your part.

Strategy 11 – Pricing

When did you last think about the prices you charge?

I know, business is tough these days. It seems like customers continually grind you down on price.

But that's not always true. It depends on how well you think about the problem from your customer's perspective.

Your pricing should be determined by what your product or service is worth to them, not what it costs you to make.

Sometimes you need to help your customers work that out, though.

For example, when I worked in the printing industry it cost £200 per hour to run one of our highly sophisticated printing machines. If a machine stopped working and it took 24 hours before we could get the part needed to fit it we'd lose £4800 of productive capacity...more if the breakdown had a knock-on effect to the workload of the downstream departments who relied on getting the work printed before they could do their part of the process.

If the downstream departments were idle too, the cost was a multiple of that initial £4800.

And because we were tight on capacity anyway, most of the time stoppages would almost certainly trigger weekend overtime rates for the printers at 2x their standard pay. A 24-hour shutdown could cost £6-7,000 in lost production and overtime payments to catch up again.

So I gladly paid a slightly higher price for spare parts from a supplier who guaranteed a 2-hour delivery, compared to the 24-hour turnaround most suppliers guaranteed, every time one of our multi-million-pound printing presses went down.

Why not try this yourself? You charge a little bit more for exactly the same thing. And customers are often happy to pay it, like I was in the example above, because of the time and money you save them in the long run.

There are lots of ways of pricing based on value. That's just one example. We cover some more in our Cash Flow Mastery programme — more details on that towards the end of this book.

The key is to think about the problem from the customer's perspective. Then work out how you can package whatever you're already doing at a higher price, while providing greater value to your customer at the same time by saving them a headache or reducing their costs without affecting your income...and often even increasing it.

Get that right and even the most tight-fisted customer will gladly pay more than they're paying now. First time round you might need to talk them through the business case from their perspective, but after that, they'll gladly pay up, putting extra cash into your bank account time after time in return for little or no extra work at your end.

Time investment: A couple of hours to think about how your service can be structured to reduce costs in your customers business, even if you charge a little bit more than you do now.

Cash investment: Often zero, but where there is an extra cost for your business, it's usually just pennies on the dollar compared to the extra income, so don't be a skinflint. This sort of offer is usually immediately cash generative and doesn't cost you a penny until a customer places an order.

Strategy 12 – What's in stock?

If you're like most businesses, the answer is "far too much".

Stock — whether raw materials or finished goods being held before getting shipped off to customers — is often maintained and topped up on a "just in case" basis. The inclination is to hold more stock rather than less because nobody wants to be responsible for running out of stock.

Fair enough as far as it goes, but every single item you've got in stock has been paid for with cold, hard cash from your bank account. That's money in your suppliers' hands rather than yours.

Because a lot of stock tends to be kept on the "just in case" basis, there tends to be a lot of wastage in there too. A lot of things get bought which won't be generating income for you for quite some time, if they ever do.

For most practical purposes, you probably don't want to run your business with no stock whatsoever — although some businesses do precisely that very successfully. But you can get pretty close to "no stock" if you put your mind to it, dramatically reducing the amount of cash you need in your business and reducing the risks production techniques might change or customers decide to deal with one of your competitors instead.

30-40 years ago, the major Japanese motor manufacturers perfected "just in time" deliveries from their suppliers. They only bring in goods an hour or two before they go on the production line.

Admittedly, they've got enormous purchasing power and can pretty much dictate terms to their suppliers in return for contracts worth $100 million a year plus. But you can do something similar.

The question to ask yourself is not "how do we make sure we never run out of stock?" as that pretty much guarantees you'll spend more of your hard-earned cash on stock than you need to.

Instead it's "how can we organise our logistics to make sure we get the product we need for our customers fast enough to respond to our customers' orders?"

If you need to get components delivered quickly, and pay "extra" for doing so, under traditional accounting methods that tends to look more expensive than if you'd bought a bulk order months ago "just in case" and had kept them in stock ever since. But that tends to look cheaper if you only consider the unit cost of whatever you bought.

Think about the cash which went out your bank account two or three months before it needed to so the supplier would send you the stock in the first place.

Think about the overdraft interest you've had to pay because you didn't have the cash in your bank account to pay for it up-front.

Think about the increased insurance for your stock — that's usually based on total stock value, so you've been paying extra to carry that stock longer than you had to.

Think about the risk of a fire destroying the warehouse and you being out of pocket for months while an insurance adjuster argues about what it cost you and tries to screw you out of every penny to agree a settlement...and so on, and so on.

In traditional accounting, stock is treated as an asset.

From your bank account's perspective, stock is just a cost, pure and simple.

There are plenty of ways to get the goods you need without holding them in stock first, or at least to get pretty close to that ideal.

Think of it as a logistics problem, not a "how do we hold stocks of everything we might possibly need in our warehouse" problem, and you'll get a different set of answers.

That way you keep a lot more cash in your bank account for longer, saving you money, keeping you cash positive.

Time investment: A couple of hours to think through the logistics and find suppliers prepared to deal with you in a way that allows you to minimise the amount of stock you hold without any impact on your ability to serve your own customers.

Cash investment: Zero — in fact you're laying out less month by month because you're buying in smaller quantities and reducing the peaks of purchasing which strain your cash flow the most. And when you factor in the true costs of holding stock, you can often pay a little more on the unit cost and still save money overall.

Strategy 13 – Office costs

Where are your offices? Swanky locations cost a lot more than offices on industrial parks.

Unless you're running a boutique, City law firm which needs to work cheek-by-jowl with the major investment banks, you don't need a swanky office unless you just want to feed your ego.

But while you're doing that, there's something more important you could be feeding instead — your bank account.

Take the opportunity to think radically about the space you need too, if you're going to move anyway.

If you've got 10,000 sq. ft downtown, in this day and age with more remote working, homeworking and the like, maybe you could get away with just 5,000 sq. ft somewhere else...or 7,500 even...all at much lower rates per square foot than you're paying now.

You might be reluctant if you think you might need space for expansion (which you should be thinking about if you put all the ideas in this book into practice as you'll soon have plenty of cash to invest in growing your business).

However, you can still go through the exercise to slim down to, say, 5,000 sq. ft at first and at the same time agree a first refusal on the unit next door, or one across the car park, for another 5,000 sq. ft when you need the space to grow into.

That way, you save twice —firstly by reducing the amount of square feet you need. Secondly, by paying for what you need at industrial park rates, not prime real estate rates. And you do so without hampering your prospects for future growth.

To sweeten the deal still further, for new leases on commercial buildings, landlords will often offer a rent-free period as an incentive to move in, which will more than cover any costs of moving, reprinting letterheads and business cards, etc and leave a bit more besides.

All the cash you save can go straight into your bank account to use as you choose, instead of paying a higher rent. You reduce your costs today with a rent-free period and you reduce your ongoing costs with a smaller office which costs much less per sq. ft than you're paying for your current offices.

Time investment: An hour or two with some commercial property experts to find you a more cost effective, but still professional, set of offices that project the right image for your business at a big saving on what you're paying now.

Cash investment: Zero — this puts money back into your bank account through the rent-free period on a new lease and ongoing rent savings.

Strategy 14 – Review your bank and finance arrangements

In my work with entrepreneurs, I often find that in the past they've arranged a series of point solutions to deal with each individual issue as it comes along.

Old machine breaks down — we lease a new one via the seller or manufacturer.

Need a new commercial mortgage — we start with our bank and quickly go to a broker in frustration at the bank's customer service. The broker pair us up with a lender we've probably never heard of, or dealt with before, at what sounds like a competitive rate.

Thinking of factoring or invoice discounting — do a quick Google search and get whoever seems cheapest to handle that for you.

Now, I'm not being disrespectful to business owners here. They're all busy people with plenty on their plates already.

But odds are, if you've got three or more financial products, all with different providers, you will probably save money overall by getting all your financing needs served by the same finance provider.

They'll all do deals in return for a wider chunk of business than they would if they were asked for each element as a one-off. So you get a better price.

Watch out for this trap though — the basis for your decision is the total cost to your business over the term of the agreement, not the individual cost for each strand of financing.

Some business owners begrudge paying, say, an extra quarter-point on their mortgage with a different provider, but don't factor in a significant saving in machine leasing or invoice discounting.

Treat all your financing as a package and you could make big savings.

Nowadays, many providers will buy you out of your current arrangements, cover your legal fees or allow you to spread the switching costs, so it really is something that quickly turns cash-positive if you get better terms in return for approaching lenders with a package of different financing needs.

It takes very little time to try. And if nobody can improve on your current terms, at least you know you're getting the best deal possible in the market and can move on to some of the other strategies for generating a cash flow surge outlined elsewhere in this book.

Time investment: 1-2 hours to speak with potential funders and see what they have to offer. (Pro tip — don't forget to ask your current providers, as long as they can cover the range of products you need. Sometimes they'll price even more keenly than a new provider to avoid losing some of the business they already have.)

Cash investment: Zero usually, although sometimes there are some modest up-front costs, depending on whether any new provider will cover switching costs or let you finance them in some way. However, make sure you build any upfront costs into your switching calculations to make sure whatever decision you make puts more money in your bank account every month than your current arrangements.

Strategy 15 – Outsourcing

Outsourcing can be a great way to get a high-quality service on a different basis to the way you pay now.

A business owner I know employs an in-house team to generate sales leads for his business. They do a reasonable enough job, but they get a salary every month whether or not they bring in any work (and if they do bring in some work, they get a bonus).

Another business owner I know has a very similar business need. But he outsourced his work to a specialist lead generation company. He only pays for each lead delivered. And in his business, which has a lot of peaks and troughs in demand for their products, this makes a lot of sense.

In quiet months, he's not putting an extra strain on his cash flow by having a bigger salary bill to pay. In good months, he's happy to pay the outsourced provider because they're generating the sales which pay the lead generation company's invoice...and even then, he only has to pay on a success basis, so he knows he's getting value straight from the off.

Either way, whether they're busy or quiet, he comes out ahead!

Nowadays you can get all sorts of services on a "pay by results" basis.

Those services also make internal costing models easier to handle. The second business owner described above, for example, knows exactly what the cost of a lead is to him. It's the cost he pays the outsourcing company, pure and simple.

Whereas the first business owner gets tangled up in all sorts of assumptions about how productive his staff are, how he can get his staff to generate leads more cost-effectively, whether or not the leads are decent quality leads or they're just names the lead generation team put forward to meet their quota for the month, and so on.

In months when it's quiet, the lead costs for that business owner are high, as there are fewer leads coming in at the same salary cost as he pays every other month. Although admittedly they're lower in busy months when his sales team is rushed off their feet with lots of leads and broadly the same total salary cost as quiet months.

So which cost would you put into your costing model for a lead?

Business Owner 1 can never be sure. Business Owner 2 knows exactly.

If you're going to make a change, there are sometimes severance costs to factor in — those will depend on the legal and contractual position in your jurisdiction.

However, many outsourcers will take on your current staff to make sure there are no severance costs to pay or cover any severance costs within their contract in return for your business, which minimises any immediate cash hit to the business.

Often when people thing about outsourcing, they think about reducing costs. And that can happen too, of course. There are usually cost savings to be had compared to doing everything internally.

But don't forget to look at the terms of service. An external provider on a "cost per lead" basis is a very different business proposition than a team of people in your business all picking up a salary whether or not they've generated a single piece of business that month.

You've got no risk with an external provider as you pay them nothing until they come up with a lead. With an in-house team you've got all the normal risks of employing people, plus the risks that they don't come up with enough leads or the leads they do come up with aren't of sufficient quality.

How you choose to manage that risk can save you cash. When money's tight and business is quiet you've got a smaller payroll to make when you outsource on a payment by results basis. You keep much-needed cash in your own bank account instead of paying it out in salaries if business is in the doldrums for a little while.

Time investment: A handful of hours in each area to identify your current costs and explore what potential outsourced suppliers can do for you.

Cash investment: Zero — but make sure you factor in the full costs of an in-house team, not just their salaries. Employers' NI, pension costs, facilities, the cost of a PC, specialist software and the many other things your staff need to do their jobs properly, their salaries are usually just a fraction of the total cost of employing someone.

Strategy 16 – Workforce balance

Even though outsourcing can be a great solution, you need to stay dispassionate.

Sometimes it makes more sense to bring services back in-house again, especially at the end of an outsourcing contract when you can do so without penalty.

You need to work closely with your CFO to make sure all the ins and outs are covered, but the basic maths goes like this.

If you've got, let's say, a Marketing Manager who works for you as a contractor, you'll probably be paying them two or three times the salary you'd pay to a full-time in-house person. But as you're not using them 5 days a week you get a better quality of marketing manager at a similar cost to a more run-of-the-mill full-time one within your existing cash budget. That can be a very smart decision, because you get so much more in return.

Perhaps they're a more experienced person...a candidate you might struggle to attract to your business for a full-time role. Perhaps they're filling in time between jobs or want to manage their workload around childcare or caring responsibilities.

Whatever your reason for outsourcing, you're not being taken advantage of by contractors in this situation. They have all sorts of out of pocket costs to pay, like an office, computer, travel expenses, insurances, licencing costs, etc that you would have to pay for a full-time person in-house. However, most companies don't join the dots to realise it costs a lot more than just the top-line salary you pay to employ someone.

At some point, though, there's enough work that needs doing to make much more sense to bring the service back in-house again and employ someone full-time.

As a portfolio Finance Director and CFO, I tell clients if they're using my services for three days a week or more on a regular basis, they should really give some thought to employing someone in-house for about the same total cash cost they're paying me.

That's better for the business because they get 7-days-a-week service for the same money they were paying for 3 days. And it's better for me because, frankly, I don't want a full-time job or anything close to it. I'm happier working for lots of different businesses on a regular basis.

If you're outsourcing anything, whether that's professional services like accounting, marketing and HR or back office services like call centres, catering and office cleaning, don't forget to check from time to time that you wouldn't be better off taking the services back in-house again.

Especially if you've been outsourcing for some time, that could well be true. And it might just cut down the monthly bills you have to pay, leaving more cash in your bank account every month than you have now.

Getting the right mix of resources to maximise the cash flow in your business is vital. That's why it's one of the components of our Cash Flow Mastery programme (details at the end of the book).

If you can keep the same level of sales, but require less resources to make those sales, the saving boosts your cash flow and puts cash right back into your bank account. Equally, if you keep your costs the same, but deliver 50% more sales...or 100% more...or 200% more...with the same cost base, your cash flow multiplies many times over.

Getting the right resources in place at the right time is one of the secrets to maximising the cash flow into your business.

Time investment: A couple of hours per outsourced service to investigate which course of action would be best for your bank balance.

Cash investment: Zero to find out if the finances make sense. There might be some legal expenses to make sure contracts are sorted out, if you haven't done that already, and perhaps some recruitment costs if your outsourced staff don't transfer to the in-house roles. You need to build a business case on a case-by-case basis, but again make sure to factor the switching costs into your financial appraisal to make sure you're doing the right thing by your bank account.

Strategy 17 – Cutting the cost of one of life's certainties

Benjamin Franklin said the only certain things in life were death and taxes. I can't help you with death, but I do have a view for you on taxes — get a review of your tax position from someone who specialises in your particular situation.

Most business owners I know just go to the nearest accountant or use the person they've used for years to file their tax return. I'm not knocking any of my professional colleagues, and accountants will have a broad understanding of the tax position most taxpayers are likely to face.

But business owners sometimes have highly complex tax situations and the more unusual your circumstances, the more likely it is a specialist can help more than someone you've picked at random or who you just happen to have worked with for a number of years.

I know tax advisors who specialise in high net worth individuals, land agents, lawyers, the music industry, manufacturing businesses, high-tech companies...the list goes on and on.

In each area, not only will they have a more in-depth knowledge of the minutiae of the tax rules and regulations than their high street cousins, they'll also have a broader base of client experiences which adds significant value to the advice they give you.

Of course, they'll preserve client confidentiality, but they'll be able to bring in their learnings from handling a successful claim on an almost identical project for another client. Applying what they learned about that earlier claim means you can "bake in" the outcomes you want now, saving you tax down the line with very little effort on your part.

It's only fair to say that the more specialist the advice, the fewer people there are providing it and the higher the charge-out rate is likely to be.

But any decent professional advisor will be keen to demonstrate a positive RoI on your spend, especially early on, because what they really want is a long-term income stream for acting on behalf of your business.

Sometimes they'll even work on a "no win, no fee" basis at first or perhaps in return for just a nominal up-front cost to cover their out of pocket expenses on the first job for you.

Either way, track down a tax specialist who is intimately familiar with your industry. Ask friends, competitors and other professional advisors. Lawyers, in particular, tend to be good about recommending highly specialist firms of accountants, as they've often come across them working for other clients themselves.

The right sort of business tax advice is worth its weight in gold.

And a pound you don't need to give to the tax authorities is another pound in your own bank account.

Time investment: An hour or two to call friends, competitors and lawyers for recommendations. Perhaps another couple of hours to brief whichever provider you choose.

Cash investment: No win, no fee is always possible — ask, and you might be pleasantly surprised, especially if you're a new client and they're keen to demonstrate a positive return on your initial investment.

Otherwise, the cost will be whatever their rates are — but bear in mind here that it's not what it costs you that matters, it's how much they save you. I'd pay someone £10,000 to save me £50,000 in taxes every day of the week and I wouldn't be griping that it cost me £10,000. I recommend you do the same.

Strategy 18 – Are you claiming all your expenses?

This strategy is less about saving your business money and more about saving you money personally.

For entrepreneurial businesses run by its owner, you need to think about not just the cost to the business, but the total cost to you.

For example, if you have an expense you pay for out your own pocket which would be a perfectly legitimate business expense it's costing you more than it should.

Anything you spend from your own pocket has already had tax deducted — depending on your income, that's somewhere between 20% and 45% for UK taxpayers as I'm writing this, although please check the latest rates, and applicable laws in your jurisdiction before taking any action.

Spending money out your own pocket on things you can legitimately claim as a business expense makes no sense as you're paying it out of cash that's already been taxed at 25-45%...and you've also missed an opportunity to claim back the VAT in that situation as you can't claim that back as a private individual.

The net effect is that your business costs do go up, but your personal expenses go down a lot more. And in a business run by the owner, that's just as good — perhaps even better.

In practice, people tend to be quite good about claiming back the specific things, but if you work from home, for example, you can legitimately claim a proportion of your housing costs. Perhaps you have some life insurance you've been paying for years which your business could legitimately pay instead. Equally pension contributions might be better structured as a company pension scheme and ease the strain on your personal finances.

These can be complicated areas to get right, so you should take appropriate professional advice before taking action. But I have seen business owners hundreds of pounds a month better off in their personal bank accounts following those strategies and getting better cover for their pensions and insurances into the bargain.

When it's your business, and you own all the shares, one way or another the profits are all yours. So, doesn't it make sense to think about which expenses your business can legitimately pay for, reducing your tax bill in the process, and allowing you to keep as much cash as possible in your personal bank account?

Time investment: A few minutes to go through the last few months' statements from your personal bank account. Are there any regular payments in there which could be turned into company expenses? Have you made any one-off payments from your personal bank account which could reasonably be refunded by your business?

Cash investment: Zero.

Strategy 19 – Selling old stock

We talked about not buying stock you don't need in Strategy 9. Here's the other side of the equation — selling any stock you've already got which isn't selling as quickly as it should be or, indeed, at all.

As we said before, some businesses buy stock in large quantities because the "per unit" cost is lower. However, if that means it sits around your warehouse longer, one way or another you've probably spent just as much as you would have done buying a smaller quantity at a higher cost per unit.

Stock costs a lot more than most people think, and every penny of it is cash out the business.

So, if you've got old stock — stock that's been knocking around your warehouse for a while - here's what to do.

Really focus your efforts on selling it. Talk to your customers about it, print up a flyer about it, put it on special offer, promote it on the front page of your website…anything you can think of to get it sold.

Do that religiously for a month.

And at the end of that month, if the stock hasn't sold, accept it probably never will. You've tried everything you can, you've promoted the living daylights out of it, you've left no stone unturned.

Now you know for certain that the stock you were keeping just in case a customer wants it is in fact stock no customers want. Unless a lottery-winning set of odds somehow works out in your favour, that stock item will still be there in a corner of your warehouse at the end of civilisation.

Now you can be secure in the knowledge that you tried everything you know to shift it, sell it.

Sell it for what you can get. Scrap it, melt it down and re-manufacture it into something else. Whatever you have to do. But get rid of it to realise some cash and stop the warehousing, insurance and storage costs mounting up for those stock items.

Your stock isn't one of your children. If too much of it hangs around for too long, get it shifted. Then don't buy those items again unless you've got a back-to-back customer order to fulfil so you don't get caught out twice.

Every penny you make is another penny back in your business, more cash back in your bank account. And if you've taken a loss on your stock sales, that will come off this year's profit and you'll end up paying less tax as a consequence, which saves you money too.

Time investment: An hour or two going through your stock lists to identify stock items which have been in the warehouse far too long and coming up with an action plan to get them shifted.

Cash investment: Zero. In the wild and whacky world of traditional accounting, someone's going to tell you that you've "lost money" writing off the stock. But you haven't really – if it was never going to sell anyway, what you've done is release "dead" cash back into your business for you to use where it's needed the most.

Strategy 20 – Automation ain't all it's cracked up to be

In our digital world, we're always being told to automate, computerise and systemise everything we do "because it's more efficient".

There was a time that was a decent enough rule of thumb. But I see plenty of clients whose business would run at a lower cost if they automated less. They pay expensive licence fees, support costs and software development costs but they've automated too much and now all that automation means it's costing them more than it should to run their business.

This lesson hit home for me years ago when I saw a video of a high-tech Japanese car factory – I think it was Honda — with impressive computer-controlled systems and robots ferrying car parts about.

Every so often there was a station where a load of people jumped all over the car, like a colony of ants finding a discarded ice cream cone on a summer's day, fiddling around inside the vehicle right next to all those fancy robots.

The person who showed me this video explained this was the "hidden secret" of low-cost Japanese manufacturing.

They'd worked out the things they were better off NOT automating, as well as the things they should automate. In fact, the Japanese manufacturers considered this a skilfully designed answer to the complicate problem of motor vehicle assembly, as it resulted in the lowest overall unit manufacturing cost.

Western car companies were so transfixed by the possibilities of automation that they automated all sorts of things that should never have been automated, robbing them of a return on their investment.

I've been known to take clients back to doing things with pen and paper for a while to make this point, and to allow them to take a more considered view of what to automate.

My current favourite target is CRM systems, especially those which are highly customised at great expense. If you're a huge company, spread across multiple sites, an all-singing, all-dancing CRM system might be unavoidable for reasons of practicality, if not RoI.

But for most businesses, you could get the same results from your customer service people writing things on bits of paper. Yes, you might lose a little bit of data, but that's almost certainly data which either (a) you're not using now because you've got so much of the stuff to handle already or (b) it's data you could collect quite easily another way so, on its own, that's not a good enough reason to build a CRM system with all its licence fees, support costs and training expenses.

Take a look at what's automated in your business and think about how you could get a workable result from just the people working there now, without all the systems costs on top. You'd be surprised how often you can, if you put your mind to it.

This strategy is part of making sure you use your resources to maximum effectiveness that we cover in the Cash Flow Mastery programme. You're looking for the lowest-cost way of achieving your objectives, not the glitziest, if you want to boost your cash flow.

Time investment: A couple of hours to look at what's been automated in your business and think about how you could get much the same effect without a heavy investment in computer systems and software...or at least a much lower investment than you have now.

Cash investment: Zero.

Strategy 21 – Pooling your purchases

Lots of things are done better with other people. Buying things for your business is one of them.

Buying groups are consolidators who will pool together a range of requirements from different businesses and use the power of having a larger order to place to negotiate a better price for everyone. Often these work on a sector basis, for example buying laminate flooring in bulk for independent installers to fit into people's homes.

There are benefits both ways. Odds are large manufacturers don't want to handle thousands of individual accounts for small, independent installers as that would significantly increase their overheads. But they're quite happy to sell at a large trade discount via a small number of large consolidators who handle all the customer interactions.

The buying groups take a cut, but still make substantial savings for independent installers over the prices they could get from a retail outlet. So everyone's happy.

Some buying groups are particularly niche. For example, there's a buying group for Christian-owned businesses in the UK which promotes itself as "saving you money so you can spend more on your own ministry".

No matter what you do, there's likely to be a buying group that's just right for you, or at least for part of what you do (office supplies, utility costs and the like). Savings are there waiting for you, ready to put more cash back into your business.

Buying groups are set up to make it easy for you to join. Their buying power with the major manufacturers increases the more members they have, because the buying groups sends more business their way.

A bit of Google searching will quickly track down a handful of suitable buying groups for your industry...or indeed your belief system. Take a look, pick the best one, and sit back to watch the cash savings come your way in pretty short order.

Not only that — as well as getting you a better price, a buying group will save a large part of the time you spend now searching for different suppliers, negotiating prices, handling the accounts and so on. You'll be making one payment a month, not 50. Your accounts team will only have one supplier to deal with, not dozens.

Yes, you should save cost on the purchase price. But don't overlook the savings elsewhere in the business too, which might be as great or greater than the saving on the goods you buy. Capture those savings too and you're on to a winner.

Time investment: An hour on Google to find a suitable buying group for your industry or location.

Cash investment: Sometimes, but not always, there's a modest fee to join a buying group. But it's in their interest to have as many members as possible, so they tend to keep the fee low which means any upfront cost is quickly covered very early in your membership.

Strategy 22 – Extended working hours

Let's be clear, these are extended working hours you're going to pay people for. A business which takes advantage of its staff won't be nearly as good as it could be — in cash terms or in any other terms for that matter.

Especially in our "always on" digital world, there are customer benefits from operating extended hours this and promoting this valuable service to potential customers, but that's not the focus of this section.

You see, if you extended your hours of work, you'll get more done, but not all your costs will increase, even though you're open for longer. If they increase at all, many costs do so at a rate far slower than your growth in sales you generate, meaning more profits and cash flow for you.

Your rent bill stays the same whether you work 8 hours a day or 24 hours a day. Ditto your website costs. Your front-line management costs might increase slightly due to the number of extra shifts you run, but you wouldn't need two Finance Directors no matter how long you were open for.

Some other costs would increase a little. Might you use a bit more electricity, for example, by opening into the evening? Almost certainly yes, but that's likely to be a very modest increase in cash terms over what you pay now, as that's not a big cost for most businesses.

Might your machines need maintaining a little more often than they do now because you're working them harder? Again, yes. But compared to the cost of buying a new machine to double-up your production capacity, the extra maintenance costs are likely to be modest.

The net result is that once you add all the different costs together, you might be able to run your business for 12 hours a day for 20% less per hour than it would cost you to run it for 8 hours a day. You can use that saving to just do more work and bank the extra cash, or you can use this new-found "headroom" in your finances to run some promotions to bring in more business, from both new and existing clients.

And if you currently pay overtime at more than a flat rate (time-and-a-third, say, or double-time), you might even make some savings while giving your staff the reassurance of working a steady shift they can plan for, instead of sporadic overtime that might be there and might not be. They can plan their lives and their finances around their new working patterns and they're often more willing than you might immediately think to trade off occasional well-paid overtime against predictable and reliable standard rate work.

However, before you get into those conversations, sit down with your accounts from last year and have a look at the items which would cost you more if you opened longer hours. Tot up the number of hours you work now and work out the number of hours you'd have available in the future.

Divide the costs by the hours available, and you'll likely see a big reduction in your operating costs per hour of operation. The "per hour of operation" is key — your costs will go up, however modestly, but if you can spread those costs over a larger number of hours, your costs per hour will go down.

You can keep those savings or use them tactically to win new business — the choice is yours.

Either way, you get more cash into your bank account in short order without having to make any major investments in new equipment.

Time investment: An hour or two with last year's accounts.

Cash investment: Zero.

Strategy 23 – Fill up the quiet times

Unless your business runs at a steady rate day in and day out, which outside steelmaking and oil refining pretty much no business does, some days will be much quieter than others.

That's dead time you're already paying for. The salaries of your workforce, the rent for your offices, the electricity that's powering your computers and air conditioning.

As you're already paying those costs, if you get even a penny of extra revenue in those quiet times, it's pretty much all profit as the costs have already been factored into your finances.

So why not encourage your customers to use that dead time. Or do some research to find another group of customers who need your services at exactly the time when you've got spare capacity.

Get this right and you boost your cash flow for very little extra cost and effort — that's why this strategy is part of our in-depth Cash Flow Mastery programme. You're already paying for your staff and the running costs of the business. Making them productive means more cash in your bank account for little or no extra effort.

Some industries understand this better than others. For example, cinemas offer cheaper tickets on Monday and Tuesday. Hairdressers offer cheaper prices during the early part of the week than on Thursday, Friday and Saturday. Restaurants have cheaper lunch menus than evening menus.

The costs for those businesses remain pretty much the same whether or not they've got any customers. But they're all worked out how to find a level of cost that's low enough to attract a different, perhaps more value-conscious, group of customers at different times to their premium customers....and at times when their business would otherwise have had no customers at all.

To give a concrete example, a restaurant makes less profit out of a £10 lunch menu than a £25 evening menu, especially after wine is added in for evening dinners given that leisurely lunchtime is rarely acceptable in business nowadays.

But the restaurant still makes a lot more profit selling £10 lunches than they would being empty until dinner service.

All restaurants do the same thing though, because the catering industry has worked out how to make the most of a winning formula. Restaurants give diners their full a la carte menu, so they don't miss out on the handful of people who want a leisurely, expensive lunch if they happen to wander in at lunchtime.

But they also have a separate, cut-down menu of lunchtime specials for £10, the dishes for which have been chosen to make sure the restaurant is at least paying the cost of ingredients and the staff wages they'd be paying anyway. Anything over and above that is a bonus.

The chalkboard outside promotes the £10 lunchtime menu, not the £25 full experience, between about 11am and 3pm. Then they switch back for the evening service.

What about your business...are you quiet between 10am and 2pm, or during the summer, or just after Christmas, or on Wednesdays, or just after the tax season is over?

Whenever you've got a quiet time, you've got an opportunity to turn that into more cash flow for your business. It might mean finding a slightly different group of customers. Their needs usually run a little counter to those of the rest of your regular customer base. But the effort is usually worth it.

Every minute of "dead time" you fill up with paying work puts cash into your business at a time it would otherwise be costing you money.

Time investment: A couple of hours to research what potential customers might be perfect you're your business at a time it would otherwise be quiet. work out when your quiet periods are and work out how to find customers for whom those times would be ideal and develop a "tweak" to your offer for those specified times only.

Cash investment: Zero.

Strategy 24 – Using consignment stocks to keep cash in your business

Consignment stocking is where a supplier delivers stock to you without raising an invoice. Instead, they do a stocktake at the end of each month and you only pay the supplier for what you've used since last month's stocktake.

It's ideal for products you use all the time and will re-order reasonably regularly. In the past I've used this sort of arrangement for bulk chemicals and lubricants, where it's relatively easy to measure how much is left in the tank at the end of the month. It's also easy for suppliers to audit, so you can both trust the results.

As long as you've got some floor space to take in an extra couple of pallets of something you use regularly, you benefit from what is effectively free stockholding. The stock stays on your supplier's books instead of yours until an invoice is raised, but it doesn't cost you anything in the meantime.

The supplier benefits because they save on warehouse space and they know they've already "sold" the products they've shipped to you, even if the invoice itself follows along a little bit later.

What's more, you never run out of stock of anything you have on consignment, which is a big bonus if it keeps your machines running when they would otherwise have to stop until the next delivery of something mission-critical arrived.

You can get creative with this idea. Major car manufacturers use exactly this approach with many of their components. Many retailers' shelves are full thanks to supplies they've been given on consignment. If what's on the shelf doesn't sell, they send it back to the supplier and they've lost nothing.

If some of the most complex businesses on the planet can make this work, so can you.

And it means you don't need to shell out cash up front for your purchases. You only pay for what you use after you've used it, typically via a reckoning-up at the end of the month. That saves you cash and keeps money in your bank account instead of your suppliers'...which is what this is all about, after all.

Time investment: An hour or two to explore the options with a handful of suppliers whose products are suited to this sort of stockholding arrangements — ideally things you use frequently, but which have a relatively low cost per item. That way, a supplier who is giving up a logistical headache will be more inclined to play ball as there's something in this arrangement for them too.

Cash investment: Zero.

Strategy 25 – Remember that website we set up ages ago…?

If you're like a lot of businesses, you'll have an idea for something and register a suitable domain name for it. As time goes by, you never quite get around to doing anything with the idea and move on to other things.

Over time, you might have built up a range of dormant websites where you've registered a domain name but never traded or done anything with them after the initial idea.

Some of those you probably don't want to lose. While I've no idea if they've registered this site or not, if I was Cadbury's, I'd obviously want to keep the cadbury.co.uk domain. And if some years previously I'd also registered CadburyFlake.co.uk, I wouldn't let that go for any amount of money. It's too valuable and too close to my main brand.

But if I was Cadbury and some years earlier, we'd contemplated a diversification into the salty end of the snack market and I'd registered a domain like BrummieCrisps.co.uk at the time, I might be tempted to see what I could get for that.

There are specialist companies who re-sell domain names. Check Google for the current lists, and make sure you check the reviews to ensure whoever you choose is above board.

You might not get the $16 million Insure.com went for, or the $11 million Hotels.com went for, but according to GoDaddy, one of the companies active in this area, the average sales price for a domain resale is in the thousands of dollars.

Putting cash into your bank account for an old domain name you're not even using — that's got to be good for your bank balance…and you even save the domain renewal fees each year into the bargain!

Time investment: An hour to check the websites you have, but don't use. Another 30-60 minutes to choose a reseller and list your site, then wait for the cash to come in!

Cash investment: Zero.

Strategy 26 – Do it ourselves or buy it in?

Many businesses feel they have to do everything themselves, and perhaps there's some truth in that in the early days of any business. With limited budgets and little cash on hand, maybe the best solution is to do as much in-house as possible, working nights and weekends if necessary.

But as the business grows, you need to ask yourself — are you just internalising a historic cost base, or would you be better buying in some of the things you sell instead of building everything yourself.

Cost savings can be substantial. You get a share of the economies of scale generated by a specialist supplier with a bigger, more efficient production facility and you shift a bunch of your costs from internal fixed costs to external variable costs instead (which is always a good idea in any event).

Instead of salaries you have to pay every week or every month, you buy in elements of your product or service, but you only pay for them if you need them. If business is quiet, it doesn't cost you a penny whereas you'd have had to pay salaries to the people you employed directly whether there was work for them to do or not.

You also take out, or substantially reduce, the cost of stockholding, the time to handle HR issues from a larger number of people, the additional operational complexity in managing the business, and many other costs too.

Don't forget, this also applies to service-based businesses. Many years ago, when I worked for an advertising agency, we didn't have our own typesetters. That job was subcontracted to a specialist firm nearby. We could have done that in-house, but the cost of the specialist equipment and the profit foregone by getting one of our £50 per hour designers to do a job a £20 per hour external resource could do just as well instead meant the smart option was to buy in that service.

See what benefits there might be to your business from trying something similar, whether you're in the service sector or the manufacturing sector.

There's no law preventing you getting quotes for different parts of your production process and comparing them to your current costs.

I'd normally start with production areas which require a lot of manual intervention and have a decent-sized staffing base. Or perhaps they have a volume of activity, for yourself and other customers, which allows them to justify a capital investment you could never hope to afford on your own.

If that's the case, odds are they'll be manufacturing a lot more cheaply than you could ever hope to.

So give it a try. You could keep a lot more cash in your business, and free up time for you to grow your business faster, just by running your business with some bought-in elements to supplement the elements you take care of in-house.

What are you doing that someone else could do for you, to at least the same standards and at a lower cost because they can access economies of scale your volumes of activity don't permit?

Time investment: An hour or two to identify areas worth costing up and getting some quotes for having that work done externally.

Cost investment: Zero.

Strategy 27 – Create an in-house out-house

I know that sounds a bit like a line from "Nutbush City Limits", but this is a hybrid strategy which I've used myself in the past.

That is to get your suppliers to run a "mini factory" of their own inside your factory. They get the space for free, but provide their own staff, equipment and supplies.

What that allows them to do is manufacture on your site relatively cheaply, because they're not paying rent. However, you benefit from not having to invest in your own people, your own stockholding and your own raw materials supply.

Combine this with the "pay only for what you use each month" approach outlined in the consignment stocking strategy above and some special prices to reflect the fact that you're effectively giving this supplier a long-term supply contract and you could save a substantial amount of cash.

You also get no stock-outs because the stock is always there, and no machine downtime due to a lack of materials. This also works with service businesses — in addition to the manufacturing experiences I had, I've seen design businesses sitting inside printing businesses, for example, and highly specialist lawyers from a different firm sitting inside other law firms to prevent the second firm needing to find extremely scarce specialist talent which they couldn't keep occupied full-time.

This approach can work in many organisations, at least to some extent. Again, it costs nothing to have a conversation with a current or potential supplier to explore the options. You're not committed to anything just by asking.

This approach works best when the in-house facility can provide a product or service you need quite frequently, even if not all the time. For services you only need once in a blue moon, it's unlikely your supplier will be able to make that into a cost-effective proposition for you.

But if there's a deal to be done, you save yourself cash, time and energy, as well as making your business more efficient, so it's worth a conversation or two to see what options there might be to save money and put more cash into your bank account.

Time investment: An hour or two in conversation with current or potential suppliers.

Cash investment: Zero.

Strategy 28 – Facilities Management

If you directly employ all your facilities support teams, it's quite likely you can outsource a lot of this and save yourself a fair bit of cash.

Admittedly this isn't the "sure fire" decision it probably was 10 years ago. In the UK at least, minimum wage legislation, TUPE laws (which govern what happens to staff when their functions are outsourced) and a range of other provisions have increased costs for outsourced service providers compared to directly employed staff in recent years.

But, depending on your situation, there could still be savings to be had. And many providers will absorb the up-front TUPE costs, redundancy costs, etc and pass that back through their monthly service charge, so you're not making any big out-of-pocket payments at the start of the relationship.

Here's why outsourcers can often save you money — they need to be really efficient in their operations to make any money. I know that because I used to run an outsourcing business myself.

We invested in sophisticated systems to become more efficient. We did predictive analysis to identify when costs might be coming our way and took early corrective action to put things right at a small cost, rather than wait until something broke and put it right at a much higher cost later. We maximised the efficiency of our workforce. We consolidated all our clients' buying power together to do much larger deals with our service providers.

We left no stone unturned to reduce our operating costs because anything we could save against a fixed monthly bill to the client was an improvement to our own bottom line.

We would also use those efficiencies to fund more attractive pricing and introductory discounts which brought new customers on board.

And that's why you might well get a good deal for your catering, cleaning, maintenance, gardening and other facilities-type costs from an outsourced service provider. It's their business to be mega efficient in areas like cutting the grass, for example, and even if you had the time and expertise to work it out, unless grass cutting is in fact your main line of business, that's an indulgence at best and a colossal waste of time at worst.

Where most businesses make the wrong choice about whether to outsource or not is in comparing what they currently pay out in salaries now to the costs quoted by an outsourcer.

That sounds logical enough, but it's not a true comparison. Your internal salary costs aren't the only costs you pay. Employers' National Insurance, pension contributions, office costs, HR support, finance charges, management time and so on all clocks up.

At least in the UK (mileage elsewhere might vary) my rough rule of thumb is that every person costs at least 1.2-1.3x whatever you're paying them in salary — generally more for high earners with their bonuses, expense accounts, private healthcare company cars, etc on top where you might be looking at 2x or even more.

So, a deal to take over your catering service at a cost no greater than your current headline salary costs is actually a 20-30% saving in real cash terms, so probably well worth doing.

A few minutes with your payroll data and a calculator will give you an idea what your facilities management teams currently cost you. Then you'll know in an instant if alternative providers are going to save you cash every month compared to what you're paying now.

Time investment: An hour with your payroll data and a calculator.

Cash investment: Zero.

Strategy 29 – Simplify purchasing

For many businesses, the purchasing processes are some of the last things people think about. Yet they're probably costing you time and money right now due to the level of management oversight, paperwork processing and administration typically involved.

There's nearly always some hierarchy of who can sign off what amount of spend, which department head can sign off for petrol for a delivery van but not petrol for a company car and all sorts of anomalies. All this takes up time, money and effort you could better deploy elsewhere.

For both manufacturing and service businesses, you can set up simple re-ordering systems which work pretty much automatically and go through your purchasing systems like a knife through butter. Ideally, those end in an automated payment (e.g. charge to a company credit card or a direct debit) to reduce purchasing administration still further.

There is a little bit of set-up to be done on this and I'd recommend piloting the concept in a non-mission critical area of your business first. But assuming it works for the trial, the same approach can normally be used elsewhere in your business quite easily.

Here's an example.

Imagine you need to order letterheaded paper for your company's correspondence. There are 500 A4 sheets in a ream of paper, usually wrapped for you by the printer, and you order 2,000 sheets a time for a sensible unit price which is four reams.

All four reams go on the shelf in the stationery cabinet and when the final ream is taken from the storeroom, an automatic re-order is triggered, ideally by a junior admin person who charges the cost to a company credit card. The printer delivers a fresh batch of 2,000 letterheads a day or two later, well before the last ream is used up, and the company can continue operations with the minimum of fuss.

Almost everything you buy in and frequently replenish can be set up to be re-ordered like that. The saving in time for the purchasing department, procurement team, managers elsewhere in the business, the finance team and everyone else involved is small per item, but across lots of items it makes a big difference, and cuts down on the non-value adding administration and paperwork that swirls around your business right now.

In the short-term, you save costs. In the longer-term, a better run business with managers who aren't spending their time on trivial things will achieve more and generate bigger profits because they have the time to focus to what really matters to the bottom line, instead of being preoccupied by relatively minor administrative tasks.

Complexity — whether that's in purchasing or elsewhere in your business — comes at a cost. Simplifying everything you do takes out complexity and that takes out cost, which means more of your income gets to your bottom line and, ultimately, your bank account.

That's why simplifying your business is another element of the Cash Flow Mastery programme.

Making it simpler to run reduces the amount of time you need to spend looking after the nuts and bolts of your business, increases the amount of time you can spend taking your business forward and boosts the amount of cash flowing into your bank account.

While your competition slowly strangles itself with bureaucracy, red tape and complex administrative procedures, you're busy taking your business forward and generating more cash flow than they ever will. Full details on our Cash Flow Mastery programme can be found at the end of this book.

Time investment: An hour or two to identify and pilot some areas to trial.

Cash investment: Zero.

Strategy 30 – Stop ranting, start fixing

Often when something goes wrong, people start shouting and blaming others. This is fundamentally counter-productive on many levels.

But the biggest problem this causes for your business is that after the rant is over people forget about it and try to put it behind them. That's dangerous, because it means the exact same situation can happen again.

People were so traumatised by the original outburst they try to forget about it, or they become so indifferent to someone's ranting they don't even listen anymore. Either way, it's a destructive move.

The biggest single contribution I've ever made to the bottom line of any business I've run has come from a continuous improvement approach which calmly acknowledges problems, large and small, as they arise and immediately sets out to find a way to ensure those problems don't occur again.

On occasion, broadly similar things can sneak through even when you've done that, in which case you just tweak the original solution to cover the combination of circumstances you didn't consider first time around and keep going.

And if exactly the same problem arises again, the solution first time round probably wasn't quite right for some reason, so go back around and try to get a better fix second time.

But keep going, whatever you do. Be calm and humble. Acknowledge that you might have contributed to the problem by not giving clear instructions, or by setting up competing priorities for staff without realising it.

Fixing the problem means reducing credit notes to customers, cutting down on overtime necessary to put things right, minimal customer complaints, reduced headaches for you and the rest of your management team so you can concentrate on building the business and...more importantly of all...reduced costs.

There's no cheaper way to run a business than to do everything "right first time". I've saved as much as 56% in unit costs from a continuous improvement programme where we wouldn't give up until we'd solved the problem.

You might not do that much, or you might do a lot more.

But can you reduce your costs by 10-20% without too much difficulty by continuously improving every part of your operations? Almost certainly yes, even if you think you've already got a cost-effective operation.

The business where I saved 56% prided itself on its efficiency. And to a point, within the department, that was true. However, they caused problems for other departments and other departments caused problems for them which nobody spent any time fixing. That was "nobody's job", so I made it mine.

It cost nothing beyond a bit of my time once a week to sit down with the production team. Some of the quickest and biggest ways I've added profits and improved cash flow in businesses I've been involved with has been through continuous improvement. It can do the same for you.

Time investment: An hour or two a week to chase issues through. In time that will dwindle to little or nothing as you'll have fixed all the big problems for good and be keeping more of the cash in your own bank account.

Cash investment: Zero.

Strategy 31 – Where there's muck there's brass

One person's refuse is another person's source of income. You just need to join the dots to save some cash.

What by-products do you create in your processes, what waste is generated in your business, what do you do with obsolete equipment you don't use any more?

Alternatively, what things do you pay to get rid of now that someone else might take away for free for you, saving the disposal costs you might otherwise have.

Everyone has something, even if it's only old, but perfectly serviceable, office equipment which a charity might come to collect from you, either to use themselves or to pass on to people who depend on their services. Either way, this saves you paying landfill fees to dispose of old equipment so you can fit in the newer version you just bought.

Sawmills sell their by-products, like sawdust for bedding in pet rabbit's hutches, probably for more per pound than their theoretical main product of planks of wood.

Oil refineries make a lot more per gallon out of exotic compounds created during the process of making petrol than they do for the petrol itself.

Copper mines often recover substantial amounts of gold and other metals as by products from their main business of copper mining.

Fast food joints sell their used vegetable oil for making into biodiesel.

You might do none of those things, but it shows the range of possibilities. Almost anything you're going to throw out, burn, destroy or send to landfill has a use somewhere else for someone else.

If that saves you the cost of disposal...or better, makes you some cash income on top...that's all extra cash in your bank account instead of someone else's.

And the beauty is, you don't need to buy anything else. This is about minimising the disposal cost of things you already have, but don't need any more. There's nothing to buy, and only upside from giving it a try.

Time investment: What do you dispose of regularly now? An hour or two's thinking can turn what is currently a cost for you into additional revenue or reduced cost by selling or disposing of things you don't need any more in a different way. Whether you increase revenues or reduce costs, either way, your bank account sees the benefit!

Cash investment: Zero.

Strategy 32 – If you don't ask, you don't get

Always ask for a discount. Whether you get one or not doesn't matter. But you don't need to win them all or enter some testosterone-fuelled negotiating session for you to save a decent amount of cash.

Some clients feel a bit awkward asking for a discount, but that's something I rarely do in quite those terms.

That's because in a lot of businesses, somebody other than the person you're talking to has to approve discounts. That builds in delay, you don't know when or whether they're going to come back with something. And you might make the person you're speaking with feel bad because they can't help you, so they'll be more reluctant to meet with you in the future.

Here's what you say instead.

In a calm, non-confrontational way, once your supplier reveals their price, just ask "is that the very best price you can offer?". Then shut up and don't say another word until your supplier speaks.

Sometimes you'll get a "yes, it is" response. Other times you'll get a "well, we could do it for a bit less, but you'd need to agree to a, b and c." Sometimes you'll get a straight "how does a 5% discount sound?"

Of course, it's up to you whether agree to any conditions they might set in return for a price reduction. Worst case, you've always got the price they originally quoted you anyway on the terms they offered back then.

Better case, you've saved a stack of cash along the way.

What's more, you'll have done it by opening the door to your supplier about how they can save you money in a win-win sort of way. If it costs you nothing to make that trade, or you're giving away something of little consequence to you in return for big cost savings, then why not?

Sometimes, you might have been happy with a 5% reduction, but because you're working with a good person on the supplier's side, they've worked out a way to get you 10%.

How you ask for a discount matters. Don't make this a purely price-based tussle and you'll often do better than you'd secretly hoped for all along.

Always ask but do it nicely. This is one area where the nice people really do win in the end.

Time investment: A minute or two tacked on to the end of a meeting you're having anyway – effectively nothing.

Cash investment: Zero.

Strategy 33 – It's a bonus for them, but is it a bonus for you?

Particularly if you employ salespeople bonuses are a big issue. Sometimes other people in a business pick up bonuses based on sales, production or profits too.

Frankly, I'm not a huge fan of bonuses. You can employ a £15k person with a £5k bonus and it will cost you £20k in total. Odds are, you'll have a much better business employing a £20k person off the bat and paying them a straight salary.

The power of bonuses to improve productivity is one of the biggest myths in HR management.

But in some sectors, or for some roles — especially salespeople —you might have little choice in practice.

What's vital, though, is making sure the bonus is calculated at the right level. That's harder than it sounds if you don't have a detailed cost structure breakdown in your business. I've had clients who have seen their profits go down as sales went up because they hadn't worked through the consequences of their bonus scheme in enough detail.

In one case, the business's star salesman — who, frankly, never wasted an opportunity to tell the MD how brilliant a salesperson he was — got paid more in bonuses for hitting sales targets than the incremental profit earned from each additional sale he made at one point.

It's easy to think that's unusual, but it's surprisingly common because few businesses understand the way costs really work in their operations. Sales is a simple metric to calculate a bonus on as it tends to be a pretty firm number in most businesses.

But it's often the least accurate number to calculate bonuses on, especially if the bonus escalates at different points along the way, e.g. 5% on sales up to £1 million, 7% on sales between £1 million and £1.5 million, and so on. There's likely to be some point, even if the 5% base rate was fair enough, that additional sales means you pay out more in bonus than you make in extra profit.

I've seen that too often to think this is a rare phenomenon. Take a look at any scheme you run which is based on sales or achieving a particular level of production output. Do you really understand the impact on your bottom line from triggering those bonus payments?

If you do, you're a rarity amongst businesses I've worked with. Most say they do, but when I do the analysis for them, they say "Gee…I never realised how we shoot ourselves in the foot by selling more and making less profit…"

So even if you think your sales bonus and production bonus schemes aren't a problem, statistically, from my perspective, there's an 80%+ chance they're not as good for your bottom line as you think, especially once you factor in all the costs of running your business.

Get out a piece of paper and start to map out all the costs in your business and how they change as sales or production increases. Then think about how much "real" profit there is on the extra sales you make once you flex the costs to match the extra activity.

Mapping all this out is one of the elements of our Cash Flow Mastery programme. Getting the business model right so that people only get bonuses when profits genuinely increase is vital if you're going to make more money and boost your cash flow.

Many businesses wonder why they always seem to be working harder, but not seeing results improve as much as they hoped…or even improve at all in some cases. The answer to that is always in the business model — get that right and managing your cash flow becomes a whole lot easier.

Cash Flow Surge

Full details of our Cash Flow Mastery programme are at the end of this book. This goes beyond whatever you get in your monthly or quarterly accounts because not all costs in a business behave the way an accounting textbook says they do.

Get under the skin of that yourself, or with the help of our Cash Flow Mastery programme, and you might make entirely different decisions.

Time investment: An hour with a piece of paper and a pen, and a copy of your most recent accounts.

Cash investment: Zero.

Strategy 34 – Cash is King...always has been, always will be

A common example of where people get bonus schemes wrong, as promised above, is not thinking about cash. Even if you go further than most people do and pay commissions and bonuses on profits rather than sales, even that isn't the best metric to use.

Think about the economics of this. If you pay cash out of the business, but don't have any extra cash coming in, those commissions and bonuses are coming straight out of your own back pocket.

At some level people usually acknowledge that, but I've often seen businesses working harder and harder, paying sales commissions to the sales team and production bonuses to the factory, rushing around to provide a great service and taking on extra admin staff because of how busy they are...all to deliver goods to a customer who doesn't pay them. Or if they do, it's six months after they should have done.

Almost without exception, those same customers are also the ones which batter you down on price or demand special favours you don't give anybody else.

These are the sort of customers you can nearly always jettison without a second thought. Whilst I suppose it's possible, they could be turned around, I've never seen it work in practice. There are some leopards whose spots just can't be changed.

Once a cheapskate, always a cheapskate. Once a late payer, always a late payer.

"How will we survive without Account X — they give us so much business?", I'm sometimes asked.

There is where a bit of analysis comes in useful. When you realise how little you get back in return from all the extra cost and aggravation, most businesses find they're better off without them. Their finances improve just by spending less in overtime in the factory, or less incurring less interest on their bank overdraft, or reducing their customer service costs.

There are some subtleties to this approach, and I normally use an advanced accounting technique called Activity Based Costing to figure out the true costs of serving each customer. But you can get a pretty decent view of whether you want to keep a customer or not just by looking at how quickly they pay you.

At the moment, interest rates are at or near historic lows. That won't last for ever, and if base rates return to anywhere near their historic average around 5-6%, with your bank's margin of 2-3% on top, there are plenty of customers who just don't generate enough profit to cover the extra costs they force your business to incur, never mind the additional financing costs you're bearing to support them.

Late payers are nearly always bad news, even you don't do a more sophisticated analysis. Identify the worst offenders and have a think about what they really cost your business – overtime in the factory, more frequent deliveries, greater customer service costs and more bank financing costs.

They might not be as much of a "great catch" as you'd been thinking all these years.

Time investment: An hour or two to identify late payers and their true cost to your business.

Cash investment: Zero.

Strategy 35 – Would you like to go large?

Next to "would you like fries with that?", "would you like to go large?" must have driven more profits into fast food joints than just about anything else McDonald's, Burger King and KFC have done.

The extra cost of popping a few extra fries into a slightly bigger carton...I'd be surprised if it was a penny or two at most. Same for the larger drink that comes with the meal. Yet each one they sell means another 50p or more in their tills. Their margins on the upsell to a larger meal are somewhere north of 90%, which isn't the sort of business opportunity you see every day.

So how do you make this approach work for you?

We cover pricing in-depth in our Cash Flow Mastery programme, but people will always pay more to get more if the offer is pitched right. Or at least some of them will.

Not every customer needs to say yes to deliver a nice chunk of 90%+ margins into their business from the ones who do.

The starting point is to think about which additional products or services could you bundle with what you do already.

Maybe, like the fast food giants, it's a simple as providing what you do already in a bigger container, priced in such a way that the extra quantity is insanely profitable for you.

Maybe you need to come up with a "super-premium" offer like, for example, personal attention instead of going through the grind of a soul-less customer experience.

Personal shoppers in swanky stores are a great example of this. You might not pay an extra fee for their services, but I'm prepared to bet people go away having bought a lot more outfits a lot closer to their full retail price than someone just browsing the rails is ever likely to do.

All you need to do is give one of your team the job of visiting your premium customers taking their instructions personally, overseeing the entire production and installation process and ensuring every detail is taken care of.

You're limited only by your imagination. It's always worth testing a super-premium offer as long as it doesn't cost you significantly extra to deliver it and the margins over and above the levels you'd expect from your standard customers are highly appealing.

You also get some useful market research information as part of this process.

For example, if a significant proportion of your customers take you up on your super-premium offer then you've probably been under-pricing your offer all along.

If that happens, take what you thought was your premium offer and make that your "standard offer". Then look to build a new super-premium offer than goes far beyond even that. Rinse and repeat this process for as long as significant numbers of clients take the upgrade package.

Once you're somewhere in the 10-20% region of people taking your super-premium offer, that's probably about right in the long term and indicates a good match with the market's price expectations and ability to pay, and your point of maximum profit-making. (Please bear in mind this is a very rough rule of thumb — you should really model it within your business to make sure this works for you economically.)

The object here is not to be greedy, but to try different ways to serve your customers better and provide them with additional services they value, appreciate and are prepared to pay for.

Get the pricing right and this is one of the quickest and easiest ways to add a significant amount of cash to your bank account.

Time investment: A few minutes every not and again to think of ways to add more value to your customers at attractive margins and pilot your offer to get some real-world feedback on how it impacts customer behaviour.

Cash investment: Zero.

Strategy 36 – The cut-down offer

I know I've just told you the importance of having premium offers and charging extra for them, but it's just as important to try the other way too, and have a cut-down, no-frills offer as well.

You do need to be careful here. This is most definitely not about cutting prices on what you do. That's just madness.

The cut-down offer involves developing a new offer in which you take some elements out your current offer, allowing you to reduce prices because your costs are also lower. Your target is to reduce the price charged to customers by less than the cost of the elements you've removed, which means your profits increase.

A cut-down offer can also be helpful for bringing new customers into your business. New customers are often understandably nervous about whether a new supplier is going to offer good value, whether the products or services are right for them, and so on.

One way to get new customers on board as customers is to have a relatively inexpensive cut-down offer so there's very little risk for them from trying out your services.

The mistake many businesses make is to cheapen their product to make the numbers work for them, but that's entirely the wrong approach — after a cheap, unimpressive customer experience you're going to have a real challenge converting the people who took a chance on your cut-down offer into repeat customers of any sort, never mind interesting them in your premium-priced offers down the track.

Whilst the customer's initial investment might be lower than your standard offer, to get the stream of profits and cashflow this strategy opens up for you, the cut-down offer must represent excellent value in its own right, even if the way it does that is different from your standard and premium offers.

You can also use this strategy to generate some windfall cash profits in the short-term. In fact, this could make a nice little nest-egg for your business which you can use to invest in some of the other strategies in this book.

What you do is you take your cut-down offer to customers you've recently missed out on doing business with and tell them about the new, high-value offer you've developed at a lower price point. Presented in the right way, some of them will buy and then you can start to migrate them towards the more expensive items in your portfolio for extra profits and stronger cash flow.

You don't, however, want a bewildering array of different products and prices. That benefits no-one, and especially not you.

There may be exceptions, but I always suggest three is a good number...a standard offer, a super-premium offer and a cut-down offer.

Broadly that's what supermarkets do — a "basics" range, a normal own-brand range and a "Taste the Difference" or "Finest" version.

Supermarkets tend to be great places to look for customer buying behaviours as they're regularly testing and experimenting with ways to get us to buy things that are most profitable for them.

If those three different tiers are the model that works best for them after decades of consumer testing across hundreds of thousands of stock lines, it's probably a model which will work out best for you too.

Consider a range of different ways to build a still-attractive offer to the client which is profitable to you at a lower price point than your standard offer — a smaller pack-size, digital-only products to save printing costs, 7 day delivery instead of 24 hour delivery, delivering training by Skype instead of in a classroom.

Build something and fine tune it until you hit upon something a reasonable proportion of your target customers buy. There are dozens of ways to develop a different offer at a lower cost.

And it will bring in customers, and cash, from places you weren't expecting faster than you might have thought possible.

Time investment: A few minutes here and there to develop an offer and try it out on a few customers to see if it gets the results you were hoping for, all while keeping your brand values and profitability intact.

Cash investment: Zero — and to the extent you use this approach to bring customers who said "no" to you first time around, your cut-down offer brings in a substantial cash injection for your business, just from thinking a little differently about your customer offer.

Strategy 37 – It's better with two

Forming partnerships and alliances is one of the quickest, cheapest and easiest ways to increase your sales, fill up your productive capacity and see more of your cash dropping into your bank account each month.

Often, these won't cost you a penny unless and until your partner delivers, making this a low-risk, high-return strategy for boosting your cash flow.

Whatever the commercial arrangements might be, a "sales force" you only pay when you make a sale can only be a good thing — that's why alliances and partnerships are part of our Cash Flow Mastery programme.

Sometimes the sale will be made by your partner, perhaps because they combine whatever you provide with something they offer, in which case you need to track the sales and make sure you get paid on time.

Sometimes you'll make the sale and give your partner either their share of the proceeds or a fee per sale, depending on what you agreed at the outset. However, if you're in charge of the selling process, I'd recommend your agreement states any fees or commissions due are only paid when you get the cash in from the end customer to make sure you're never out of pocket.

The only limit to a potential partnership is in your own imagination. If you make photocopy paper, for example, you might partner with an installer of photocopiers for them to leave, at no charge to their client, a box of your copy paper with your name, phone number and re-order details prominently displayed every time they install a new machine.

If the business which bought the new photocopier re-orders some paper from you when the sample batch is finished, you pay a small commission to the installation company.

The net cost to you for supplying a free box of copier paper — perhaps a pound or two.

Let's face it, you'd never be able to make a sales call for that amount of money, and most sales calls don't result in a sale either, even though they cost a lot more than a couple of pounds.

So even a relatively small proportion of photocopier installations turning into long term customers for you means you earn a positive return on your modest investment as well as gaining a new customer you might be able to sell a range of other products and services to in the future.

That pound or two up-front could earn you thousands over the lifetime of that customer relationship. And best of all, you didn't need a single salesperson to bring in that new customer.

When you can generate new revenues at little or no up-front cost and get a steady stream of long-term customers out the process, there are few easier ways than that to grow positive cash flow than partnerships and alliances with complementary businesses who supply the same customers you'd like to have for yourself.

Time investment: An hour or two thinking about who would make a good partner for you (ideally someone who has an existing relationship with the customers you're targeting) and making a few phone calls.

Cash investment: Little or nothing, depending on how the deal is structured. But even with a small up-front cost, like in the box of photocopying paper scenario, a steady stream of new business on the back-end means partnerships and alliances are a great way to improve your cash flow at little or no risk or cost.

Strategy 38 – Partnerships work both ways

Like a good marriage, partnerships work best both ways, and potentially further reduces your up-front cash outlay to bring more cash into your business.

In the previous strategy we talked about how partnerships can work for you, but what about if you partnered with another business where you have existing customer relationships, but they don't.

To extend the example above, what if you were the photocopier installer? Could you find a paper supplier and offer to do the same deal for them, in return for a percentage of their income from any client you introduce them? I bet you could.

For you, it's an easy sell. More or less all you do is take along a box of your partner's copy paper every time you do an installation. Your partner has supplied that to you for nothing, so you don't need to charge your customer for it.

You use one of the reams out the box to do your test prints to make sure you're handing the photocopier across in good condition.

When your engineer is collecting the client's signature to confirm they've happy with the installation, you might get them to say something like "I've left you a box of XYZ's copy paper for you to use at no extra charge. We always use them for our test prints because they offer good quality at a reasonable price. If you like using their copy paper, re-order details are printed on the box in the cabinet underneath the machine."

For extra points, you might have some stickers printed up, at your copy paper supplier's expense, with the reorder details on them and make sure your engineer sticks one somewhere prominent on the copier before they finish that installation and head on to the next one.

This takes you and your engineer no time at all. There's no extra effort and no extra cost. Your engineer is already on the client's premises talking to the person in charge of ordering photocopiers and copy paper. The extra couple of seconds it takes to direct the client's attention towards XYZ's copy paper has an effective cost of zero.

But for the customers who order that copy paper as a result of your introduction, you get a nice monthly payment for each customer every time they re-order some copy paper.

Go on — have a think about who might benefit from the customer relationships you've painstakingly built up over the years and reach out to a few. The cost to you is next to nothing. The upside, in return for almost no work at all, could be considerable.

Time investment: An hour or two to think about who you could help to build their own business via a partnership with you, in return for some commission or a flat rate payment for you every time you help them make a sale.

Cash investment: Zero.

Strategy 39 – Trial offers to find new customers cheaply

Should you be unlucky enough to have spare capacity in your business, why not use it to generate some future cash flow for your business?

If you set this up right, after covering production costs, the benefit drops straight to the bottom line and into your bank account.

The way you do it is by creating a trial offer, designed to appeal to potential new customers. This is covered in more detail in the Cash Flow Mastery programme as trial offers, when they're done right, are a great way to use up spare capacity at the same time as building your future revenue streams and cash flow.

Please note, I said "trial offer", not necessarily a free offer. Although, depending on the type of business you run and the proportion of direct costs to total cost of production, you might want to consider one of those too.

Here's how a trial offer works.

Imagine you're already paying your staff salaries, whether or not they're fully engaged on work for paying clients, and the direct external cash costs of your product or service is 50% of the sales value. To attract new customers without any negative impact on your bottom line, you could therefore offer new customers a "50% off trial", which would cover the additional external costs without being out of pocket (beyond the salaries you'd be paying anyway).

Your business is cash-neutral in the short-term, as the additional costs are covered by additional revenues. But when the trial ends you shift to regular pricing and your income then increases by the 50% difference between your external costs and your normal selling price.

Remember you're still paying your staff whether they're fully occupied or not, so all the extra added value you bring into the business through this route is cash profit.

At some point, when everyone is busy 100% of the time, you only make whatever your normal profit margin is. But up until that point, your cash flow is better off by the difference between the extra sales revenues and the additional costs for materials or services required to make those sales.

The terms for trial offers vary widely — first order at 50% off, first 30 days at 50% off and all purchases by XYZ date are popular formats — but the right answer for your business depends on your industry, your cost structure and what, if anything, your competitors do.

Properly structured, trial offers are great for both cold leads and people you've been courting for a while. They bring in more customers at little or no net cost. At least a proportion of those customers will keep buying from you in the future after their trial period ends, bringing in an additional stream of profits and cash into your business in pretty short order.

Time investment: An hour or two to work out the level at which you can afford to pitch your trial offer — 50% off or "buy one, get one free" is the sort of territory you need to be aiming at. It needs to seem like a great deal...5% off is unlikely to cut the mustard with potential new customers.

Cash investment: Zero — cash neutral on "hard costs" in the short-term, with unlimited cash generating possibilities in the long term as a stream of new customers come through.

Strategy 40 – Logistics

Logistics of one sort or other stymies many an otherwise fine business.

That might be inbound logistics, it might be outbound logistics, it might be internal logistics. And this applies for service-based businesses too, not just firms which move things around the country by truck.

In most businesses, many different elements need to come together in to create the product or service you sell to your customers. "Logistics" in this context means whatever those mission-critical things are for you — property searches for a law firm, the latest colouring kits for a hairdresser, and so on.

For your business to be efficient, and generate as much cash as possible, your people need to focus on the job in hand, serving your customer. Every moment they step away from their machine to find something, ask a question or make a phone call is non-productive time. It might be necessary on occasion, but that should be rare and in most businesses it's anything but.

Getting logistics right means your people spend more of their time generating income for your business, which in turn brings in as much cash as possible.

One business I ran had a logistics problem in the factory when I started there. People spent huge amounts of time trying to find the components they needed for the next job on their machine and were only doing chargeable work around 76% of the time.

Whilst 100% productivity might sound ideal, that's unrealistic for most settings. And for us, because we ran 24 hours a day, we needed to allow time for maintenance and staff training as we couldn't do what other firms did and do the maintenance at night after the machines had finished for the day.

By the time I left we were up to 87% productivity, and on track for 90%, which I reckoned was about the maximum we could hope for. That might sound like a bit of a gap from 100%, but with the maintenance time required on our machines, that was a great result.

Even 87%, though, was 14.4% more productive than the 76% we'd been at before. That's nearly 15% more work going through the factory with no increase in staff costs, no increase in machine costs and no new capital investments.

Don't forget, we were already paying the staff for their shift whether the machines ran or not. So that extra 15% productive time, after the costs of direct materials, all flowed straight to our bottom line and put cash into our bank account.

What we did was very simple. Any business can do this.

Every time someone had to leave their machine to find something or do something, the manager asked what problem they were trying to address and then let them go and do whatever they needed to do (we still had customers to satisfy, let's remember).

At the end of every week, we looked at any reasons which came up more than once or twice and fixed whatever it was. (Fixing the "once or twice" instances were how we were going to get from 87% to 90%, if I hadn't left in the meantime. But we started with the more frequent causes of delay.)

It couldn't be simpler or cheaper to implement. Often the problem was a communication issue where one department didn't realise the issues their working practices were causing for another department. Those could be fixed there and then for an investment of nothing at all.

Simplifying your business operations is key to improving your cash flow. That's why it's part of the Cash Flow Mastery programme. Simplifying procedures and eliminating costly errors means your costs reduce, leading to more cash flowing into your bank accounts instead of flowing our to patch over problems.

Finding out where your logistics are letting you down, and fixing whatever the underlying reasons are, is a sure-fire route to greater productivity without spending any more cash. This means you make more profit, generate more cash and increase the financial return from the people and machines you're already paying for.

It's easy to fix. Just start somewhere and don't let up until there aren't any more issues to solve.

Time investment: 5 minutes a day to ask, "what's got in the way of you being as productive as possible today?". Then fix whatever that is — probably another few minutes. Rinse and repeat until there aren't any more issues to solve.

Cash investment: Zero.

Strategy 41 – Smart people don't take shortcuts

There's nothing more expensive than a short-cut.

Unless you're a shady, fly-by-night, cut-and-run merchant, which I'm sure you're not if you've been smart enough to invest in this book, doing a job properly first time round is always the point of maximum profitability for your business.

It's also how you generate the maximum amount of cash possible. No more paying people to come in at overtime rates on a Saturday to fix a problem the business caused itself the previous Wednesday. No more credit notes to customers for late or wrong deliveries. No more tax inspectors crawling all over your business and taking the time you could have spent generating more cash with their audits and questions.

No short-cuts are always the smart solution.

When I was a boy accountant, I was greatly influenced by Philip Crosby's book "Quality Is Free", which became something of a mantra in the early days of the quality management revolution.

And he wasn't wrong. If your business can save the costs of putting things right which should never had gone wrong in the first place, you'll save a fortune.

If a product is shipped without some bit it should have had inside, that costs you money.

As do the things that were finished a little slap-dash just so they'd make it to the loading dock in time for the truck, but which are sent back by the customer a few days later to be finished off properly.

As do the times your client gets product A when they should have had Product B, because your order-picker wasn't paying attention, or your labelling wasn't as informative as it might have been.

Same goes for the service industry. If a lawyer loses a case on the technicality because all the evidence wasn't submitted to the court on time or the wrong forms were completed, their clients probably won't be coming back for legal advice any time soon.

If your client's haircut isn't quite right, but they don't notice until they get home, you're going to have to fix it.

If your taxi goes to a similar sounding, but incorrect, address to pick you up, the taxi driver will spend more money on more petrol getting to the pick-up point than if they had gone to the right address in the first place.

The possible causes are endless. But this really is a "less haste, more speed" situation.

Get the haste vs speed balance right first time and you eliminate substantial costs from your business.

Do that consistently and more of the revenues coming into your business will stay there, boosting your cash flow and making sure you keep more of your hard-earned cash instead of wasting it on overtime, extra delivery charges, and the cost of putting things right which should never have gone wrong.

Make this one of your priorities, as we cover in-depth in our Cash Flow Mastery programme, and you'll quickly reduce the cost of errors in your business, including the errors nobody is telling you about at the moment. That means you costs reduce and your cash flow increases, putting more money in your pocket.

Doing it right first time is the lowest cost way of running any business. That's why quality is still free…and it helps build customer loyalty and brings long-term cash flow benefits into the bargain.

Time investment: Spend 10 minutes today finding out what things happen in your business which bump up your costs — the extra deliveries, the re-work, the credit notes issued to customers when things haven't gone right.

Each day pick one and fix whatever the root cause might have been to make sure they never happen again. Do that consistently for a few weeks and you'll catch most of the big ones.

Cash investment: Zero — no upfront costs, and when you stop spending money you don't have to, you get to keep all the cash you currently spend to put things right.

Strategy 42 – Increase your prices

You might think I've left this strategy a little late in the book.

However, I'd argue that until you've done some other things to make sure your business is running more effectively, you're on a much dicier wicket trying to increase prices to your customers.

It's obvious when you think about it.

Of course, nobody likes price increases. But if you have to concede one from someone, who gets the nod...the business which can't seem to get a delivery organised on time and has to re-work what they supply on a fairly regular basis, or the business with a 100% on-time, 100% error-free track record?

I know the one I'd be conceding a price rise to. And I suspect you'd be the same, so don't be surprised if your customers think the same way.

Also don't be surprised if your customer's initial reaction to you wanting to raise prices is "no" or "I'll go somewhere else".

Frankly some will, but by and large they are cheapskates your business can do without, so don't shed too many tears.

This is also the reason why you should introduce price rises gradually, so even if someone does take their business away in a huff, it's not fatal for your operations. (If you've applied some of the strategies in this book so far, and developed a more finely tuned business, old customers might come back when they've had a chance to find out how much poorer your competitors are than you, anyway.)

Price rises are always really good for your business and are much better in profit terms and cash generation terms than reductions to your own costs. Here's why.

Let's say you get a 10% price reduction to your most important purchase which accounts for 50% of the costs of your business. That only increases your bottom line by 5% (10% times 50%).

Increase your prices by 10% and, without any increase in productive capacity, greater labour costs or increased material costs, that flatters your bottom line, and therefore your cash position, by 10% - double the impact of cutting costs.

It's never easy to persuade customers to accept price increases, but it's not impossible either.

Even if not everyone agrees, or if you concede for a couple of particularly valued customers that you'll hold prices at current levels, for those who do accept a price increase you can still bank the extra profit those customers generate.

If even a single customer agrees to a price increase, that means more cash staying in your bank account than there was before. And it cost you nothing beyond the cost of a letter or a quick phone call.

Different businesses will approach this in different ways.

If you have a large number of small customers, all it probably takes is re-issuing your price list or updating your website with the new prices.

If you've got a small number of large customers, you might want to try a more softly-softly approach, which is the subject of our next strategy.

But I can't emphasise enough that you're in a weak position if your quality and service isn't all it could be. The likelihood of your customer allowing you to increase prices in return for poor quality and unreliable service isn't high.

Put that right first and earn a reputation for being a well-organised, reliable, cost-effective supplier. You might be surprised how often you can get at least some extra cash in your bank account for doing no more than you're doing now.

Don't be greedy, even a couple of percent each year brings in more cash for no more effort, and that fresh surge of cash into your bank account kicks in as soon as you implement the new prices.

Even if you think none of your customers will wear a price increase, it's worth making the effort to ask as it's easy extra cash in your bank from whenever your new prices kick in.

Getting the pricing right is so important to your cash flow, it's one of the key components of the Cash Flow Mastery programme. You can find full details at the end of this book.

Time investment: A few minutes with your accountant to work out the impact on your profit margins of putting up your prices, followed by a few minutes more to decide when and how you'll try to introduce any increases to maximise the effect on your bottom line and your cash flow.

Cash investment: Zero, with a great RoI from the customers who accept an increase. Once your new prices are implemented, the extra cash starts flowing into your bank account more or less immediately.

Strategy 43 – The cash flow benefits of value engineering

Have you noticed what all the consumer products businesses have been doing lately? Pack sizes have been changing.

Smaller bars of chocolate and slimmer cans of soft drinks have been introduced by the major food brands recently to minimise the impact of the UK's new sugar tax.

Washing powder companies now offer plus-size value packs and mini-sized travel packs, liquid detergent as well as powder detergent and so on.

The cheese I buy in Tesco which used to come in 500g packs has started to come in 460g packs.

Let me tell you now, not a single one of those ideas is implemented unless the consumer products business is confident their profits will go up rather than down as a consequence. And if initial market testing suggests it doesn't, the new product is swiftly withdrawn before too much damage is done.

There are several different flavours of this. Sometimes manufacturers offer less product at the same price...the favoured strategy for chocolate bars as far as I can tell. Net result - bigger margins and better cash flow.

Other times they offer more product at a higher price, perhaps twice as much product for only 50% more. You think you're getting a bargain as the unit price, or the price per kg has gone down substantially. But the reality is the consumer products business has spent only pennies more. It's the retail world's version of "would you like to go large?" in the fast food restaurant, and just as insanely profitable.

£5 for 100g vs £7.50 for 200g makes the latter sound like a bargain...even if your marginal costs were only an extra 50p to generate an extra income of £2.50, and a profit of £2.

Major retailers and consumer product companies are world-class experts on how to get the maximum amount of cash out their customers' wallets for selling them the exact same stuff. There are plenty of ways of getting your customers to pay more without realising it.

And if you're smart about it, your customers might even think they're getting the bargain of the century, although the truth is it's the seller's profits which are being boosted here, not the buyers.

Go for a walk around your nearest large supermarket and pay special attention to their offers. Compare them to the "standard pricing" and how prices and pack sizes for different brands and quantities compare. That will give you plenty of ideas you can work into your own business.

There's no need to pay for a lot of expensive research, just look at what the world-class experts down your local supermarket already do and take some inspiration from them — the precise details will need tailoring to your own business circumstances but the concepts in plain sight down your local Tesco adapt just fine to almost any business.

Even a few extra pennies here and there flow straight through to your bottom line and boosts your cashflow.

To give just one example, Tesco made £2.2bn operating profit last year by getting good at the psychology of how to merchandise what they sell. That might be a stretch for your business right now, but you can make significant improvements in profits and cash flow by following their example.

Time investment: An hour to walk around your local supermarket

Cash investment: Little or nothing — the modest cost of any changes you might make, such as new packaging, will have a more or less instant RoI so you'll be cash positive very quickly.

Strategy 44 – Annual hours

Annual hours is a great strategy for keeping the lid on overtime costs.

Nobody who gets overtime pay would willingly give it up without some persuasion, so this has to be structured as a win-win for both parties. However, I made this work very effectively, even in a highly unionised environment, because the union were happy to support the win-win deal I proposed.

Here's how it worked.

We paid our staff for 35 hours a week over (to keep the maths simple) a 48-week year. That means we paid for 1,680 hours a year at standard time and everything else at either time-and-a-half or double-time, depending on a range of circumstances. In practice, most people worked about 2,000 hours a year, so we paid more than the standard rate for about 300 hours per person per year on average.

But here's the thing about overtime. Not only is it voluntary for the member of staff, the business isn't obliged to offer any overtime either.

My proposal was for a deal which would guarantee a certain number of hours over the course of the year, provided they were structured in line with seasonal client demands on our business and the machines kept running year-round at full pelt. This was to make sure our staff couldn't work 20 hours a day in the first few months of the year and take the rest of the year off.

This extra pay was guaranteed, unlike overtime, but only at standard rates. That way we could remain competitive in a tough market and give the staff earnings they could count on alongside the ability to organise their own workloads and spend more time with their family.

Whilst I acknowledged all those other benefits, I made no secret of the fact that we were doing it primarily to reduce costs. I didn't want to be seen as some smooth-talking huckster with our workforce. I wanted them to understand exactly what the benefits would be to them, and the downsides as well.

In the end, the workforce was happy to trade more hours in which they were guaranteed to be earning, and appreciated the flexibility to work those hours around their interests outside work, in place of overtime that they could never depend on and which wouldn't be counted for their mortgage and pension benefits.

The net saving was substantial and whilst for really excessive hours we did in practice pay a small honorarium to recognise the individuals' contribution over and above the call of duty, we took a historic overtime bill of between £250k and £500k a year and translated that into "over and above the call of duty" payments of less than £30k a year.

The benefit was slightly offset by the extra guaranteed hours we were paying, but as those were all at standard rates, rather than premium rates, we were still ahead of the game by a decent six-figure sum.

More importantly, we had significantly limited our downside risk in the event of a run of bad luck on the overtime front. This protected our profit margins for the year because we had extra hours we could call on without triggering extra overtime payments.

If you pay overtime to some or all the people in your business, could you try something similar?

At first you might think "why would they agree?" but get the right deal in place and you can make your workforce happier and more productive at a lower cost, while they benefit from a higher level of guaranteed income and improved pensions.

It's worth a conversation, at least. Your workforce might surprise you.

Time investment: This might take several conversations over a period of time. It isn't a quick fix, but you can start these conversations while implementing some of the other ideas in this book. By the time you've improved your cash flow using some of those other strategies, this one might just be the icing on the cake.

Cash investment: Zero — there's no cost to asking, even if the answer's "no". And there's potentially big savings if you get the win-win deal right.

Strategy 45 – "Free" email costs you a fortune

Forget everything you've been told about email being an efficient way to communicate.

A study by elite global consulting firm McKinsey, quoted in the Harvard Business Review, determined that professionals spend an average of 28% of their time at work writing or answering emails.

Might you need to spend 5 or 10% of your time on emails...well, perhaps. But nearly a third of your time at work...11 hours or so out of a 40-hour working week...seems way out of kilter with any benefits you might be getting.

People are swapping a 2-minute phone call for the 15 minutes it takes them to type and proofread an email.

Other people hide behind emails to save them having difficult conversations face-to-face.

Still others fritter their time away on things that don't matter, but because they're always busy tapping away on their keyboard everyone in the office, including their boss, thinks they're being highly productive.

There isn't a direct cost-saving, as such, from the approach I'm going to tell you about. But there is a massive opportunity cost saving — that is, they could be doing something much more productive with their time instead.

Here's what to do — start doing more things in person.

Hold a short morning meeting with your team to make sure the plans for the day are on track.

Pick up the phone to that customer or supplier rather than send an email. Especially for customers, the tone of your communication is very hard to pick up in an email. You wouldn't be the first supplier whose humorously intended email mortally offended a valued customer. Talk to them on the phone and you'll stand a much better change of gauging the mood right.

Make a point of walking around the office and checking in with people in person every day. Make it a habit and people won't come and bother you, they'll just wait till you pass by "on your daily rounds" to ask those questions they'd otherwise have interrupted you about.

Write a letter or a card by hand. Nobody gets those anymore, so a personal 1-to-1 communication like that really stands out. Done well, it's a classy way of being remembered.

Yes, none of those things are truly free, but none of them cost very much.

Whereas "free" email clogs up your systems, demotivates your people and gives anyone who wants it somewhere to hide amongst the extended email trails and the bcc's.

Get in the habit of doing more things old-style and you might be surprised how much smoother the business runs. Issues don't fester, people don't spend hours reading through long email chains, staff members don't get to hide behind their computer screens when there's a difficult conversation to have.

This is also how to free up time to implement some of the other strategies in this book. You can delegate some of these strategies to members of your team without it costing you more because you're already paying them their salaries. So if you cut out the distractions that stop them focusing on the most important jobs in your business, you'll save money now and build a cash flow surge that sustains your business into the future without spending a penny more than you would have spent anyway for your teams to spend their day just answering a few emails and hiding behind their PCs.

Time investment: Little or nothing. Eliminate distractions and you build your cash flow faster than you would do otherwise. Decisions will be quicker, and benefits will come sooner, so there are plenty of upsides and no downsides to this strategy.

Cash investment: Zero.

Strategy 46 – Do you really need so many managers?

Of course, you need some managers in your business, otherwise all the problems in the world will land in your lap instead. And, for a large proportion of those problems at least, it's not a great use of your time to solve problems others can solve on your behalf.

That said, most businesses I come across have far too many managers, supervisors, administrators and goodness knows what else.

Sometimes clients tell me they need that many managers because they have a lot of problems to deal with. Obviously, that's true in a sense. What I advise them to do is make sure those problems go away, then they won't need as many managers to resolve them.

There's a helpful framework in the Cash Flow Mastery programme for how to make sure you've got the right number of managers and administrators in your business — full details of that programme at the end of the book.

Managers and administrators are often used to paper over the cracks in business operations. Fix the problem for good and there are no cracks to paper over so you don't need as many crack-paperers, meaning you can reduce costs and improve cash flow.

For example, in many businesses a secretary or administrator takes notes of meetings, types them up and circulates them to attendees in advance of the next meeting so everyone stays on track (at least in theory).

By doing this, we also guarantee the first 20-30 minutes of the next meeting will be full of excuses as to why people haven't completed the actions they said they would at the last meeting — it's just not very productive.

If people just did what they said they would, that's one administrative role you can do without.

The best technique I've ever seen was a former chairman who took handwritten notes of action points in his meetings, along with who was doing it and by when, on a little grid he kept in his notebook. He then took a photo of the action points he'd written up and circulated that to the management team.

No typed-up minutes, no meetings secretaries, no managers, no overhead, nothing.

It also allowed him to avoid the 30 minutes at the start of the next meeting where everyone updates whatever the minutes said from the last meeting — usually some variant of "no I haven't done it yet, but I've got a really good reason".

He kept meetings short, focused them on action and held people accountable, all without a manager, a secretary or administrator in sight.

You'd be surprised how much of your management and administration costs you can reduce without any detriment to your business.

And if you can't, there's something far wrong with the people you've employed. Which might be another good reason to try this strategy out, just to see what happens.

Reduce management and administration costs — your business will often run more smoothly and the benefits of saving overhead salaries fall straight through to your bottom line.

Time investment: Little or nothing — just start running your meetings differently and see what happens.

Cash investment: Zero.

Strategy 47 – A strategic approach to purchasing

When did you last look at what you buy for your business in a strategic way?

Your accounts team will be able to get you a list of how much you've spent with each of your suppliers for the last few years easily enough.

Take a look and see what the significant spends are in there or whether there have been major ups and downs over the period.

Most businesses don't think about their purchasing from a strategic perspective very often. When the business is running out of something, they just re-order more of whatever they bought last time.

However if you've dramatically increased your spend with a supplier over the last year or two, now might be a good time to go back to them and ask for a better price, or some other enhancement to their offer, such as them swallowing the delivery charge instead of billing you for it as an extra.

Now, if the spend is up 5% year on year, you'll look like an amateur trying this, so I don't recommend it. If a big order comes along, by all means ask for a better deal at that point in time, but if it's pretty much same ol', same ol' I wouldn't make the call.

I'd also keep this to your bigger suppliers. If the corner sandwich shop has benefitted from £200 in income from you this year, and only £100 last year, don't try the "we've doubled our spend with you so can we have a better price" approach. You'll look like a prat...and I wouldn't go eating sandwiches purchased from there for a while if I were you.

Depending on your business, your top dozen or so suppliers is about where you want to be having this conversation.

For anyone you're spending, say, 20-30% more with year on year, just call them up out the blue and tell them you've just noticed you're doing a lot more business with them than you used to, and you'd appreciate them thinking about the ways they can give you a better price.

Don't ask for price reductions as such and don't be dragged into a debate about what you want or how you want it structured.

Just assure them that you value their support and service, but your margins are under pressure and you're giving them a lot more business than you used to which, you imagine, means they would be in a better position to do something for you on the total package than might have been the case when you set up the current agreement a couple of years ago.

The "total package" is key. Give them the space to come up with something imaginative as a way of keeping your business. It also gives them a way to serve you better without necessarily slashing their own margins. For suppliers you value, you need them to be profitable in the long run too, or they won't be around to supply you at any price.

Suppliers will generally be highly motived to keep a client who's growing at 20-30% a year and it's sometimes interesting to see what they come back with. It doesn't mean you have to do what they suggest, but really good suppliers will often pleasantly surprise you about the ways they can serve you better and save you money.

If they do, they're a keeper. Work closely with them over the coming months and years. They'll give you ways to save your business money and improve the service you offer to your own customers. Good suppliers really are worth their weight in gold.

Essentially you get free consultancy about how to keep more cash in your own bank account. And there aren't many better deals than that.

Go on, ask the question. It'll only take you a few minutes. You never know where it might lead you.

Time investment: A few minutes on the phone with each of major suppliers who's seen substantial year on year growth in purchases from you.

Cash Flow Surge

Cash investment: Zero.

Strategy 48 – Past performance is not necessarily a guide to the future

A great way to keep more of your cash in your bank account is to remember the past is not necessarily a guide to the future. They say that in all the financial ads for a reason.

That means when something changes suddenly and unexpectedly, your objective is not to try and recreate the world the way it used to be. It's to embrace the new reality and see how you can make things better.

For example, if a senior member of staff leaves, in most businesses the knee-jerk reaction tends to be "we need another Marketing Director" (or whatever he or she was).

If you lose the Asda account, the first thought is often "how do we get into Sainsbury's to replace that business?".

If government regulation comes along to stop you, for example, screwing your customers through selling them inappropriate PPI products, your first thought shouldn't be "how do we screw our customers in ways that don't involve PPI products?".

Most people are in a perpetual battle to reinvent the past when what they should be doing is realigning what they do to create a better future.

If someone leaves, no matter how key they were, don't rush to replace them - could you do without that post...perhaps promote someone internally without replacing them further down the organisation...consider outsourcing more of your marketing so you don't need that resource internally at all?

If you lose the Asda account, perhaps you need to think whether supplying via one of the big retailers is the best way to sell your products. There's never been a better time to go direct to the consumer with a compelling offer — and since you won't be giving a major retailer half the sales price, you can afford to undercut the high street stores and still make more money than you are at the moment.

And if regulation stops you screwing your customers, that's a good thing. You shouldn't have been doing it in the first place, of course, but take it as a warning shot. Nothing makes your long-term customer value plummet like getting a reputation for taking advantage of your customers.

Your long-term customer value, directly and indirectly, drives how much you can sell your business for and how much wealth you can generate from it.

Come up with a better way to service your customers and work to keep them for longer. There are fewer more economically sensible ways to run your business and maximise the cash in your bank account.

So, when unexpected change happens, even if that's change you'd rather hadn't happened, don't try to reinvent the past. Pause for breath…hang on to your cash in the short-term while you decide what to do.

Make the right decision for the future and you'll have a business which is more effective and efficient, putting more cash into your bank account without having to spend a penny yourself.

Time investment: Pretty much zero — just a few minutes steeling yourself not to make a hasty decision when something major changes in your business.

Cost: Zero.

Strategy 49 – Keep in contact

How often have you bought something from a business and been surprised never to hear from them again?

It happens to me a lot...and I don't think that's just because they don't like me very much...

Six months down the line when I want to re-order or recommend a business to someone else, am I likely to remember who I dealt with? Almost certainly not – I'm a busy person and, in the nicest possible way, your business is probably not something I think about day and night. I've got my own business to think about.

The cost of keeping in contact is somewhere between completely free (e.g. email) up to not very much (perhaps a stamp for a letter). But if someone remembers your business and buys again or refers you on, the upside is huge. That's why keeping in contact with your customers...in the right way...is part of the Cash Flow Mastery programme (details at the end of the book).

Don't make the mistake made by most businesses who go down this avenue, though.

Don't bore your customers to death with your own PR announcements or things that look like they were written by a robot.

Think about ways you can keep in touch as a way of enhancing their enjoyment out of whatever they bought from you.

If I bought a lawnmower from you, for example, I might appreciate hearing from you from time to time with, say, some "top tips on mowing your lawn when the grass is wet", some ideas of when the time is right to apply weed killer to my lawn, or some recommendations of how best to prepare my garden for winter.

I'm not a gardener, but if I was and, over the course of the year, I received some inexpensive communication from you every now and again which helped me with my original objective — in this case having a nice lawn — I'd probably appreciate that.

I might even pass some of these on to my brother or my buddy down the street when they were thinking of buying a new lawnmower. And when my lawnmower was due a replacement, guess where I'd be coming first...that's right, straight back to you again.

You've gone to all the effort and expense of acquiring a customer. Don't just ignore them once you bank their cheque. A happy customer means repeat purchases and referrals – the most inexpensive way to grow your business imaginable.

So keep in touch. For the very modest cost involved, you're unlikely to find a better RoI from an outlay of pretty close to zero.

Time investment: This is what your marketing team should be doing, so it shouldn't take you any time at all. If you don't have a dedicated marketing team, an office manager or secretary can do it more than adequately with a bit of up-front thinking and planning (e.g. what time of year to send out the "best time to apply weed killer" information pack).

Cash investment: Little or nothing per customer...sometimes completely free depending on how you choose to keep in touch.

Strategy 50 – Simple ways to avoid the cost of errors

You can learn a lot from the way people outside your business do interesting things.

Here's some ideas from hospitals, based on academic research which was written up in the British Medical Journal.

One of the biggest problems for hospitals is the mistakes which can creep in when nurses go around the ward dispensing medication. A moment's inattention and a patient gets the wrong drug, or the wrong dose of the right drug, and can suffer severe consequences, even death.

Leaving aside the undeniable human consequences of that moment's inattention, the financial costs in lawsuits for hospitals whose staff dispense the wrong medication is enormous.

The study in the BMJ highlighted some simple and virtually cost-free ways of reducing those errors.

Some of the errors were caused by nurses on the wards getting interrupted while giving a patient their medication. Depending on what else was going on in the ward at the same time, that momentary distraction was occasionally enough to give a bit too much, a bit too little or the wrong medication altogether to a patient.

Let's remember here that nurses are people whose life's work is to help make people healthy again. These mistakes aren't the result of deliberate actions or incompetence. They're the very human errors we all make...except most of us don't face life-threatening consequences for the moments we're gazing out the window in a meeting and not giving the subject under discussion our full attention.

So, here are some of the things that were proven to reduce errors.

When nurses were giving patients their medication, they wore a fluorescent jacket with "Do Not Disturb" printed on it so people knew to

119

leave them alone to concentrate on giving their patients the correct medication.

Sometimes when dispensing medication there was a time element involved — 10 seconds of this, 30 seconds of that, or whatever. Nurses could lose count if they were interrupted and forget the start time or the finish time. However, placing some cheap timers at each location meant they no longer had to hold that information in their minds. They could see how long they'd taken with a visible timer.

Simple checklists were also deployed, a bit like the pre-take off check pilots do. Nobody wants pilots to forget a step in a vital safety-critical process, but until fairly recently nobody thought to extend the same benefits to nurses.

As a result of these various interventions, error rates reduced dramatically, and hospitals saved the cost of compensating patients. Away from the purely financial consequences, it's also important to note that people's lives weren't negatively affected from being given the wrong dose of the right medication or the wrong medication altogether.

At one level all these strategies might seem rather obvious. But the key here is that all good ideas are obvious in retrospect — until studies into errors dispensing medication were conducted, generations of nurses were operating without anybody thinking about how to make their vital job of dispensing medication to patients less risky and more reliable.

I come across similar problems in business every day — admittedly without the life-threatening consequences nurses have to cope with.

Often you don't need some overblown process, a new manager to oversee a problem area, or issuing all staff with disciplinary notices. In fact, rarely will any of those be good answers.

What you need to do instead is to make it easier to do the right thing, rather than disciplining people after the event for doing the wrong thing. By then the horse has well and truly bolted and you're already saddled with the cost of putting things right anyway.

It's far better to stop making errors and keep the cash in your bank account instead of having to pay out to put things right. That's why simplifying your business operations is such an important part of our Cash Flow Mastery programme.

Get it right and the savings are enormous.

Time investment: A few minutes here and there to spot the issues and try some low cost or no cost ways of making it easier to do the job right than to do it wrong.

Cash investment: Zero, or pretty close to it. Any modest up-front expense, such as the fluorescent vests for the nurses on dispensing duty, will quickly be recouped through not having the significant costs of putting mistakes right after the event.

Strategy 51 – Cut out switching costs

For most things in life, there's a cost of switching from one thing to another. It's obvious in a factory if a machine has to stop running while the old tooling is taken off and the new tooling put back on again. That can take from minutes to hours depending on the nature of your operations.

It's a lot less obvious in leadership, management, selling or administration roles, but that doesn't mean the same effect isn't still there.

Every time you stop doing one thing and switch to another, you're taking up time. And you know the old expression "time is money".

If you've got 10 people in a department and they're each working at only 80% efficiency, you could in theory get through the same amount of work with two people less.

And it's not because your people aren't working hard already. They almost certainly are.

But the systems and processes just aren't as efficient as they could be. The net result is that you're spending more money than you have to on the running costs of your business.

The most efficient way to run a manufacturing operation is to set the machines up on a Monday morning and run them exactly like that all week, without needing any further intervention. That allows you to amortise the set-up costs across a larger number of units of production, which keeps your unit costs as low as possible.

Here's how to get the same effect going in your offices — get teams to specialise. Instead of everybody answering the phones at random, for example, give the job of answering the phones to one person or allocate the duty on a rota basis across the department. That person answers phone calls all day long, meaning everyone else isn't switching between whatever else they were doing to answer the phone. That in turn means they're more efficient at delivering the department's work.

The one person answering the phones becomes highly efficient at answering the phones – they get answered faster so your designated call taker can handle more calls an hour than someone who has to put their main work aside first before they can talk to a customer.

And because your designated call-handler isn't feeling interrupted by a phone call while they're under pressure to get something else done at the same time, they're likely to be in a more positive and customer-friendly frame of mind when they do answer the phone, leading to better customer relationships and more business from that customer over time.

The other benefit is that the non-phone answerers on the team can get their heads down and pile through their work without interruption.

One American Psychological Association study put the cost of switching between tasks at up to 40% of an individual's time. Multiply that across a department of 10 and you can easily see why the department might need a couple of extra people to get through its workload. Some of the reasons are more complex but often it's fast, easy and cheap to engineer out a big chunk of switching costs so that each department runs more smoothly.

Cut out switching costs and you'll do more with less resources, become more cost effective as a result and put more money in your bank account as you won't need to employ all those extra people just to get through the day's work.

Mostly, this won't cost you a penny, it's just about how you organise the people you've already got inside your business for maximum effectiveness at minimum cost.

Time investment: A few minutes per department to agree how to organise the team members to improve efficiency via specialisation.

Cost investment: Zero.

Strategy 52 – Test your way to success

Businesses incur substantial costs by doing things that don't work. They have to scrap whatever they've spent weeks, months or years developing and start again, often after incurring substantial costs in the process.

That might be a marketing campaign that doesn't work, a new product your customers hate, a strategic alliance with someone who lets you down, a new staff member who doesn't work out as you'd hoped or any one of a hundred other things.

Whatever the cause, this means money going down the drain. Money you didn't need to spend. Money that's now in someone else's bank account instead of yours.

Here's what more businesses could benefit from — testing their way to success.

Unless you're designing nuclear power stations, you've nearly always got a way to try your idea out...at a low cost or sometimes no cost at all...without risking a project that falls flat on its face and costs you thousands, or even millions.

Smart businesses test things all the time.

Got an idea for a new product you think customers might like — can you jerry-rig a prototype and let a couple of real customers have a play with it?

Got an idea for a new marketing campaign — can you try out the theme with your existing photography and copy, perhaps by just changing the headline or a few details on an existing ad to see if it hits home with customers the way you hope it will?

Want to employ a new member of staff — why not give them a trial project to work on first? Not a trial period in their new job, but something they do before they start so both you and they know they're the right fit for the role and bring the right skills and competencies. If you don't find that out until they've been with you for weeks or months, unpicking that situation will always be costly and unpleasant.

Pro tip: pay people for the trial project, especially if they're having to do it in their own time around a full-time job. It doesn't need to be a fortune, but a few hundred quid up front to avoid you getting in a situation a few months later might save you £5-10,000 in severance costs, legal fees and bad feeling all round. That seems like a good deal to me.

The smartest people I know don't put everything on the line on a single spin of the roulette wheel. They don't launch until they've trialled as many elements of the process as possible in low-cost and no-cost ways.

Now and again, their best efforts still hit the buffers, but the savings they make from not having spent a fortune on people, new products or marketing that just don't work are enormous, and more than cover the odd occasion when, despite their best efforts, somehow the final result doesn't quite hit the mark.

Even though every project isn't necessarily a game changer, the likelihood of people who test new ideas rigorously coming away completely empty-handed more than once in a blue moon is pretty low. Getting good at testing means you don't spend your hard-earned cash until you know you've got a pretty safe bet on your hands.

And when that safe bet pays off, as safe bets mostly do, you get a rapid return on an investment and a fresh surge of cash flowing into your bank account...which is what business is all about.

Time investment: You save time this way rather than spending it. Instead of huge amounts of time spent on big projects that fail, you spend tiny amounts of time testing each element, so your effort is rarely wasted.

Cash investment: Usually little or nothing – even when you do need to spend some cash (a little bit of tooling, paying for the project your potential new hire delivers, etc) that's nothing compared to the costs you'd have incurred by getting right to the end of a big project, only for it not to work and get scrapped after you've spent a fortune. There's a big RoI on getting good at testing!

Strategy 53 – Don't get sunk by sunk costs

Understanding sunk costs won't in itself save money right now, but it will help stop you throwing good money after bad in the future.

Sunk costs are the costs you've already incurred, and which won't change irrespective of any decision you make now. You should therefore ignore them in any decision making from this point on.

Imagine you bought a piece of machinery costing £100,000 which could only make a single product. Historically that product has been highly profitable, but it's now gone out of fashion. The machine's scrap value is no more than £2,000. Should you employ a salesperson at a cost of £25,000 a year to try to revitalise the market and recover the profits you used to make from this product?

Lots of people would say "I've already spent £100,000, so I ought to spend another £25,000 to try to get my money's worth out of the machine."

That is almost always completely the wrong answer.

You can't un-spend the £100,000 you've already spent, and its scrap value is negligible. The only product it can make is a product nobody wants to buy.

Although most people don't think of it this way, your choice at this moment in time is either to bank £2,000 selling the machine for scrap or to spend £25,000 a year to revive a product nobody wants to buy.

Your most profitable course of action is to sell the machine for £2,000, otherwise a year from now you'll be looking at £125,000 in sunk costs — the original £100,000 for the machine and the £25,000 you've spent on wages in the last year. And, in all probability, you still won't have sold any products, because we've already established nobody wants to buy them.

Your sunk cost — the machine in this case — should be taken out of your decision-making. All that matters is what's going to happen from here on in...a quick injection of £2,000 in cash or a further £25,000 in losses without any hope of return.

Explained like that, it seems obvious, but in plenty of businesses that's the least likely outcome of a boardroom discussion.

In management decision-making, what you've already spent is largely irrelevant. All that matters is what are you going to spend from this point onwards, and how much revenue will those decisions create. You need to separate the ego swirling around wanting to prove the original decision right from making the right financial decision now.

Getting good at spotting opportunity cost prevents you throwing good money after bad and keeps as much of your future cash flows in your bank account as possible.

Time investment: A few minutes per case to work out whether there are any opportunity costs impacting on a decision you're about to make.

Cash investment: Zero.

Strategy 54 – Outsource then hire

When business picks up, what do you do? Often businesses rush to hire more people to cope with the increased activity.

That's especially true when managers within the business have been complaining for some time about being understaffed. At the first sign of an uptick in the business all those proposals for new staff you've been putting off for a while on the basis that "we'll wait till we get a bit busier" get dusted off and the pressure on you to hire more people takes a dramatic turn upwards.

Clearly, being busier may well require more people in your business, but rarely should your first instinct be to hire new people directly. In most cases you'll be better off outsourcing your needs or using contractors or consultants to fill the gaps for a few months.

You get two major benefits that way.

Benefit one is that you can be sure the upturn in business will be sustainable over the medium term. The other benefit is that you can use this opportunity to "road test" some people you might want to offer a full-time role to once you're sure the upturn in business is here to stay.

Most businesses look at a consultant or an agency worker's daily rate and have a small seizure. But here's why that can often the best way to go.

Firstly, you don't always need the support on a full-time basis. Perhaps you need a consultant for a day a week instead of a full-time member of staff every day. Even if the consultant costs twice what you'd pay a full-time person for the day, you're still the equivalent of three days a week better off using a consultant instead of hiring.

Secondly, consultants and agency staff, in the UK at least, bear their own pension and National Insurance costs and don't get holiday pay. When you add those costs to the headline salary you pay your full-time staff, you'll discover the cost to your business of employing people directly is much higher than their salary alone, sometimes as much as 20-30% higher.

So, the true cost difference between a full-time staff member and a temporary member of staff, especially if you only need them on a part-time basis, is much less than you might immediately think.

Finally, what happens if things don't work out? We all know the costs and complications involved when you have to part company with a full-time member of staff. But with a consultant or temporary worker, you can usually end the contract without financial penalties or risk to you within a few days if your plans change, or even if you just don't like working with them.

There's also the upside of using a consultant or temporary member of staff to essentially act as a longer job interview so once you're certain the uptick in business is here to stay, you've got a great candidate already trained and someone you know has the right work ethic and attitude for your business.

Even if using a consultant or temporary member of staff looks like it's more expensive, when you add up all the costs and benefits, using a consultant or temporary member of staff is often a better, lower cost decision for the business, saving you money and keeping more of your cash in your own bank account.

Time investment: No more time than to hire the new full-time member of staff you were going to employ anyway...in fact probably less.

Cash investment: Often a net zero compared to the cost of hiring a new full-time member of staff, especially if you don't need someone with that expertise in the business 100% of the time (which, in the early stages of an upturn in business, you probably won't).

Strategy 55 – How "it's just a fiver" can cost you a six-figure sum

Delivery charges can rack up — both delivery charges from your suppliers and deliveries you make to your own customers.

One of my clients wasn't terribly bothered about delivery charges ("after all, it's only a fiver…") until I pointed out that the charges their suppliers levied, plus their historic practice of delivering orders to clients without making a delivery charge of their own was costing them over £100,000 a year.

With your suppliers, you should negotiate a price to include delivery charges to make sure there are no hidden extras coming your way. It also means when you do your costing to work out a price for your clients you know you've included the full cost from your suppliers.

It won't surprise you to know that with your customers, the opposite applies. You should always seek to quote "ex works" and add any delivery charge to your invoice, especially if clients demand express deliveries, the costs for which can quickly mount up if you're footing the bill.

You might need to change your terms of business to do this, depending on what they say now. If there's nothing specific in there just start quoting ex works from the next quote you cost up. Slip it in there without any fuss or fanfare and see what happens.

If customers make a big fuss you can always take it off again. But especially if you time this for a spike in oil prices or an increase in vehicle excise duty, your customers will often accept that you can't absorb every price increase that comes along.

Some businesses have a strict rule against delivery charges (although in truth, even businesses which say they do will sometimes pay delivery charges for mission-critical supplies and services, so don't give up even if that's their starting point in negotiations).

But you can use the delivery charge as an excuse to talk about your prices more generally — "We don't want to add a fiver on each delivery, but times are hard, and margins are getting close to nothing. Could we perhaps add a few pennies to the unit cost instead and we'll keep absorbing the delivery charges?"

Sometimes by not getting a delivery charge, you get something much better in the shape of a price increase across the board. So, it's worth having that conversation.

If you're met with a straight refusal, you've lost nothing. If you can persuade even some of your suppliers to absorb their delivery costs, perhaps in return for the increase in business from you they've seen in the last few years, then you're ahead of the game.

And if customers accept a delivery charge or a small increase to their unit costs across the board to compensate, then you're quids in.

Time investment: It takes seconds to add a delivery charge to a quote and only a few minutes per supplier to ask if they can absorb delivery charges in the future.

Cash investment: Zero — if you don't get anything, it's cost you nothing. But all those fivers add up, perhaps not to the £100,000 a year my client was originally spending, but a tidy sum nevertheless.

Strategy 56 – Technology isn't always the right answer

Technology provides many benefits, but it only works at scale when thousands of identical activities are taking place every day.

By the time you factor in the costs of developing a new system, training your staff and the disadvantages to your business of the inflexibility you're about to build into your operations, the cost of technology is high...perhaps too high.

Expensive though that is, you can make your tech solutions even more expensive if you cut corners on system design or try to force your customers to follow a process they don't find helpful (even if it might seem helpful to you, at first sight).

It doesn't take much change to customer churn — the number of customers leaving vs the number of customers opening new accounts — for the real costs of your new system to skyrocket.

Obviously the cash you spend on the system remains the same, but if you're losing customers with a potential lifetime value of, say, £100,000 each and it costs £10,000 in sales and marketing expenses to sign up every new one, the total cost of the new system quickly goes through the roof if your customers start taking their business elsewhere.

This can be a significant cost of implementing new technology and most businesses overlook it completely — yet it can be the biggest cost of introducing a new system. (You'll be glad to know that's why we cover this in our Cash Flow Mastery programme, so you can make the right decisions to maximise your cash flow.)

You might think nobody would ever set out to create a system so bad that customers feel their only option is to take their business elsewhere, and you'd be right.

But technology's "dirty little secret" is that can be the outcome when systems are over-complicated or when systems designers try to hard-wire every possible eventuality into their software. Take it from me...you could spend the next 100 years designing a "perfect" system and someone would find a way it doesn't work for them. They always do.

Instead use technology more as a way to triage customer needs than necessarily try to solve them all.

At a hospital A&E Department, they separate incoming patients into three groups — those in imminent danger of death or serious consequences who need to be seen immediately, the walking wounded who just need a stitch or two but are otherwise fine who can be seen when someone isn't busy doing something more important, and those in the middle who won't die if they're left for a couple of hours, but you'd patch them up before sewing together a cut on someone's finger.

In tech terms, you probably can triage most things. At a basic level a good FAQ (Frequently Asked Questions) page on your website, or a link to an operating manual on your site might help people find their own answers to problems.

If that doesn't answer the question to your customer's satisfaction, the tech solution might be offering your customers the opportunity to chat then and there on your website, while the problem is fresh in their mind.

The hand-off to chat can be automated, but obviously from there on in, your customers need more tailored solutions than they could find on the FAQ for themselves (don't do what one robot-powered tech chat service did to me recently and give me "answers" by sending me links to the FAQs I'd already read and found lacking — that was the height of customer service stupidity).

Finally, your chat operator might offer an outbound call from a specialist to handle the customer's query, when the business needs a more complex, more nuanced solution. Again, you can automate some elements of that handoff, such as making sure the tech specialist has access to all the chat records and actually reads them before calling back (people get cheesed off pretty quickly if they have to repeat the same story over and over again).

However, from this point onwards, don't imagine you can roll out another tech solution. The process from here on in needs a human to solve the problem if you're going to retain your customer's confidence.

Automating things that should never be automated costs businesses millions of pounds every year. If you try to automate everything, you'll pay the price — both upfront in the capital costs of developing a new system and on an ongoing basis if the new tech solution upsets customers enough that they start to buy elsewhere.

You'll save money if you consciously don't try to automate everything.

For finely nuanced, more complex issues, human beings are by far the cheapest way to serve your customers, as long as you give them the authority to provide real solutions then and there to your customers without endless handoffs to progressively more senior managers.

That way, you're more likely to keep those customers buying from your business than implementing a half-assed, all-singing, all-dancing tech solution. The way to keep more cash in your bank account is to make sure you're not forcing your customers to buy elsewhere because you force them through a technology-driven process which doesn't work for them.

The recipe for steady, reliable cash flow which increases over time is to keep the customers you already have for longer and add more customers on a regular basis. That's easier to do if you don't irritate them with tech solutions that don't work when a human being could get an answer for your customers faster, easier and cheaper.

It's cheaper for you to deliver and your customers get the answers they need faster — a real win-win!

Time investment: Little or none. You'll get new systems implemented faster by taking out the nth level of complexity, and they'll be more reliable when they're up and running too.

Cash investment: Zero. This saves you money right from the off and keeps on saving right into the future.

Strategy 57 – It's not about price, it's all about value

I wish I could remember who said this, but years ago someone told me "price resistance is more in the mind of the seller than the buyer".

What this means is that, given a choice between presenting a lower priced offer or a higher priced one, the vast majority of people will be tempted to lead with the lower price first.

There are two reasons why this isn't the best approach. Firstly, once you've "anchored" an amount, say £500, in a client's head, it will be a devil of a job to make them think some higher amount, say £1000, represents a "good deal". It will always seem like an expensive option, however well you sell it.

But if you lead with your most expensive offer, provided you've got strong value-based reasons for your service being more than worth the money you're asking for it, a surprising number of people will just say "yes" to the higher price without a further thought.

Even if they don't, rather than getting into a price gouging competition, if they raise price objections, you've got a down-sell offer already in place — "we can't do that for less than £1000, but we do have a service which is great but doesn't offer all the added features of our £1000 one, but costs only £500".

To the buyer, £500 sounds a lot cheaper than £1000, so you've already got them thinking this is a good deal and you still stand a reasonable chance of making a sale. Trying to get a customer up to £1,000 from a £500 starting point isn't quite doomed to failure, but it comes close.

A word of warning, though. You have to make sure your £1,000 product is a good value proposition in its own right, not just the sort of amateur price gouging you see on "The Apprentice" where a seemingly never-ending succession of idiots try to pass off canned tuna as caviar.

That approach works in real life about as well as it works in Lord Sugar's boardroom...which is to say it never works more than once, and most of the time it doesn't even work that often.

You can make a very nice living out of high-priced products which deliver value, and nobody will complain about your prices because they've had so much more value out of your product or service than whatever it cost them to buy it in the first place.

But don't try to scam your customers. As soon as they realise they've been had, nothing you do from that point on will turn out well for you and your business.

The only direction your cash flow is going to be surging after you pull a stunt like that is straight out of your bank account as customers leave in droves.

That's why our Cash Flow Mastery programme helps you to spot the difference between offering real extra value customers are prepared to pay for and ramping up prices so customers feel ripped off, and take their business elsewhere. Details at the end of this book.

The best way to see ever-increasing positive cash flow in your business is to offer great value at prices high enough for you to offer that extra value and still turn a profit.

Time investment: Nothing beyond the time it would have taken to present your cheapest offer first.

Cash investment: Zero. It doesn't cost any more to start your pricing conversations with your most expensive offer than with your cheapest.

Strategy 58 – Avoid long-term contracts

A business I know recently agreed a 5-year IT support contract with a managed services provider. They thought this was a good result because their supplier had started out asking for a 10-year contract.

This was a smallish growing business, so the likelihood of their IT needs being anything like similar between the time they signed their deal and a point in time even five years, never mind 10 years, later was pretty much zero. Statistically by then, they'd either be a much larger business with more complex needs than the system was designed for or they'd have shut down or sold out.

And, of course, this IT firm were deploying one of the strategies I mentioned earlier — start with their highest-price product and working down from there.

The IT firm's client was deploying a tried and trusted procurement technique, which is broadly "how low can I get the unit cost by buying in bulk or signing up for a longer-term contract?" But in the process, they'd pretty much skewered themselves by getting tied into a long-term contract they couldn't get out of if their circumstances changed.

Especially for IT in this day and age, there's pretty much nothing you can get on a long-term contract you can't get on a month-by-month or performance-related basis.

A plethora of cloud services can do most things you could ever think of, and several things you probably couldn't. Services like AWS can hold more data more cheaply than you could ever imagine for pennies...and you only pay for what you use on AWS, with no long-term contracts.

Many other IT providers have services which you can scale up or down without penalty on a month-by-month basis depending on the number of users who log on to their platform in each 30-day period.

Some IT providers even offer free trials to make sure the software works for you, often a full-featured version of the software, not just a demo system, before you spend even a penny.

Of course, IT service providers like to sell the "one stop shop" convenience of their services, but that convenience comes at a pretty steep price. Often that price is not worth paying.

Over the years, I've seen plenty of businesses paying external service providers well into six figures for IT solutions when I'd have been staggered if it would have cost them 20 grand to sort out a perfectly workable solution themselves.

Would it have been quite as slick or polished? Well, sometimes no...although more often than you might think, yes.

But would it have worked perfectly well and saved them nearly £100,000 or more every year? It certainly would.

The difference between the two creates positive cash flow for your business and keeps more of your hard-earned cash in your own bank account.

That's not only true for IT. Whatever your supplier or service provider tells you, most of the benefits of long-term contracts flow to the supplier, not to the person they're supplying. It secures the supplier's income stream and cash flow far enough into the future to keep their bank manager happy more or less indefinitely.

If they need to give you a tiny part of that long-term benefit by knocking down what they charge you by a few percent, that's usually a price that's worth them paying — what they get in return is much more valuable than what they're giving up.

When you model it out, most businesses I've come across would be better off with a short contract, even at a higher unit cost, because when something changes...as it will, sure as eggs is eggs...you can quickly shut down what you used to do and do something different instead, without worrying about penalties or long-term contracts.

The right answer for your business depends on the nature of the service and the discount you're being offered for a longer contract, but I get really twitchy at anything with more than a 12 month term, and generally try to get three or six months' notice as a maximum, 30 days if at all possible.

You should do the same if you want to maximise your cash flow.

Time investment: Nothing — you're already having the conversation with your supplier and you're bound to be pitched a range of options. It's just about the option you're going to choose, or whether you're going to send your supplier away to work up something that suits your needs better.

Cash investment: This approach sounds more expensive, but it rarely is over two or three years, never mind five or ten. The key is to switch your thinking from getting the lowest unit cost to getting the lowest total cost over the contract period, including "locked-in" periods you might end up not using. Sometimes "saving money" is the most expensive thing you can do for your business.

Strategy 59 – The show must go on

We've all heard the old showbiz expression "the show must go on". Whatever happens, that evening's performance takes place to entertain the people who've spent their hard-earned money on tickets.

But how does your "show" go on when disaster strikes?

I'm not necessarily talking about your factory going up in flames or something dramatic like that...although that might happen too.

What if your business partner passed away unexpectedly?

What if your star salesperson quits for a job with the competition?

What if the IT platform your business depends on stops being supported by whoever sold it to you in the first place?

Any business can spend for ever thinking about "what If's". But the key here is that when things happen suddenly, sorting them out often costs a lot more in the short-term than they would have done if they'd been properly planned for in the first place.

So, take a quick inventory around your business. What are the key things that would bring your business to its knees more or less immediately?

If your business is like most I come across, it probably boils down to a handful of individuals and a few pieces of equipment.

People like your Sales Director...the star receptionist who's loved by all your customers...the "mad scientist" who's happy in their lab all day inventing things for your business to sell...

For equipment, it generally boils down to anything you've only got one of or anything that has to work round the clock even though your office only works 9-5.

For example, when I ran a printing business, we needed printing plates for every job — that's how the process works. Lithographic printing needs those metal printing plates to get the right amount of ink in the right places. And we only had one platemaking machine, so if that machine broke, the factory ground to a halt.

Equally I used to work at a very sophisticated engineering firm which did structural stress testing on motorway bridges and North Sea oil rigs. They had their own in-house IT set up which processed thousands of bits of safety-critical information, but their IT system had to run round the clock to keep up with the volume of information they collected, even though the staff only worked 9-5 (apart from those in the IT section who worked 24 x 7).

The machine for making printing plates and the engineering firm's computer system were mission critical, and each was a single point of failure with enormous costs to put right in a hurry if they fell over unexpectedly.

So, don't wait for disaster to strike before developing ways to keep going if it does.

That's almost guaranteed to be an expensive way to fix anything as you'll be charged premium rates by everyone involved, whether that's the recruitment firm you engage to find a replacement for a vital member of staff who just handed in their notice or the specialist who's going to be despatched up the motorway at high speed to fix the machine or computer which just broke and brought your business to a halt.

There are always ways to save money in situations like this.

Pay your staff well and treat them well. It's a lot less likely they're going to leave you if you do. Don't begrudge paying them an extra couple of grand a year...in fact if they really are key people you should grasp the opportunity to do so because that makes it less likely they'll be tempted to work for a competitor.

Any extra spend in the short-term is more than covered by saving you a recruitment fee of 20-30% of their salary when you have to replace them...and you might even have to pay an incoming member of staff more than the one who left to attract them into your business. That's happened to more than one business I've dealt with.

And for your equipment, there's always a way round it. During my time at the printing firm, we made an agreement with another firm nearby that if our platemaking machine went down, they'd make our plates on their equipment and we offered them the same facility in return. It cost neither of us a penny for this facility and it saved us thousands of pounds for the handful of times each year we did have a breakdown in the platemaking department.

Of course, we got the machine fixed, but not at premium rates because we organised ourselves to make sure it wasn't as vital to our business as it would otherwise have been.

When you've got something...a person, a machine, a piece of technology...without which your business grinds to a halt, it always costs you less to have a Plan B for each of them than to start running around in a panic when trouble turns up at your door. When the pressure's on, most businesses make expensive decisions they live to regret.

A little bit of time working out how to make sure "the show still goes on" no matter what happens in your business will save you a fortune and keep more of your cash in your bank account for longer.

Time investment: A couple of hours working our which parts of your business are vulnerable if a person left or a machine broke. You don't need a major research project, it's just the things you're already worrying about on a regular basis, even if that's only subconsciously.

Cash investment: Zero. All you need is a pen and a piece of paper to work out what you need to do and to outline a plan for doing something about it. Don't forget barter as an option, like we did with our platemaking machine.

Strategy 60 – Consequences vs likelihood

One way businesses can save money is by thinking about what I call "consequences vs likelihood". Here's what I mean by that...

What are the odds of a 747 landing on your factory and destroying everything? Very, very, very low.

What are the consequences to your business of a 747 landing on your factory? Catastrophic.

Because events like this are very rare, insurance cover is available at very reasonable rates against that sort of risk, so it makes sense to spend £50 a year on insurance, or whatever it might be. You can afford £50 quite easily, but a catastrophic event which flattened your factory would cost you millions if you weren't insured.

When odds are low, costs are also low, so it makes sense to protect yourself by spending £50 to save millions.

It doesn't work the other way around.

Something that's very likely but the impact on your business is trivial doesn't need insuring against – especially as insurers round the world are hiking excesses on policies.

It makes no sense to insure yourself when something is very likely to happen but, when that event happens, as it assuredly will, you're still out of pocket because the £500 it costs you to put right is less than the £1,000 compulsory excess on your insurance policy.

You might think nobody would insure themselves on that basis, but I've got news for you...

When insurance agents are, by and large, remunerated at a percentage of the premiums you pay, they've got every incentive to sell you every bit of insurance they can think of.

Cash Flow Surge

They can spin you a story about how a premium of X will cover you for up to 100 claims a year...and as you know, Mr Client, this sort of claim is something every business in the country will experience several times a week.

I'm not suggesting for a moment suggesting they are anything other than sincere about the risks to your business. But very few people do the maths on the likelihood of not just the incident taking place, but the likelihood of any claim being significantly more than the policy excess.

Yes, they'll trot out horror stories about the case "just like yours" when a judge somewhere ordered millions of pounds in compensation on a business which didn't have the insurance cover they're recommending. But if the cost of fixing something is less than the amount of the excess, my starting point is that this is something I'd normally recommend a close look at.

Sometimes it's easier and cheaper in the long run just to pay out your £500s as each claim comes along than pay insurance premiums and have to go through the whole claims process with your insurers, which can be something of an ordeal in its own right.

If your insurance is protecting you against catastrophic events, then it's more likely to be worth spending your money on the premiums. Otherwise, think carefully and do the maths of the cost to your business with and without insurance...remembering that in the long run insurers need to make sure they're bringing in enough premium income to cover the claims they pay out, so the more you claim the more your premiums are likely to rise over time.

Either way, of course, a book like this can't give personal advice on your individual circumstances so make sure you get good advice from an independent fee-based, rather than commission-based, financial adviser on all your insurance policies.

Good ones will sort out the insurances you don't need, or that offer poor value, and will generally still save you money on what you're paying now, even after taking their fee into account. That's usually money well spent because you end up saving a lot more than you're spending.

Time investment: If anything, getting an expert to investigate your various insurance policies is cheaper and faster than doing it yourself, and they have a better idea what to look for. So probably a net time saving here.

Cash investment: Usually nothing up-front with any fees more than covered by savings on your insurances.

Strategy 61 – The undertaker's secret

Several years ago, I did a lot of work with a business contact whose first job was working in his family's undertaker's business.

He was a really fun guy to deal with and not necessarily what you'd expect from someone who started out as a junior assistant in an undertaker's, although by the time I first met him he'd long since left the family business to pursue a career in something a little more glamorous.

However, he once told me something very instructive — that it's very rare for people to get three competing quotes for the funeral of someone they loved.

I must be honest, I'd never thought of it like that, but he was right. It's a traumatic time for everyone involved and nobody wants to make the grieving process any more drawn out than it absolutely has to be. People select an undertaker from a quick search or the recommendation of a friend and just sign up to whatever they offer that seems about right.

Now, I'm not suggesting undertakers take undue advantage of that, although unscrupulous ones could, I guess.

But I am suggesting you ask yourself — what things does your business buy that you or your staff are reluctant to get three quotes for? Odds are those are precisely the areas where you could get a better deal.

The best salesman I ever worked with made a very nice living supplying letterheads and stationery to small and medium-sized businesses where inevitably the secretary or the receptionist was in charge of buying office supplies. There usually wasn't an in-house procurement person either.

While he didn't take undue advantage, he wooed every secretary and receptionist he could find in our town and was a genuinely nice guy who was friends with everyone. He brought small gifts from time to time, like a packet of nice biscuits or a small box of chocolates, and never forgot a birthday card or a Christmas card.

Not a single person Peter secured as a customer would ever dream of getting a quote from anyone else.

Of course, from time to time a longstanding customer left for a job somewhere else, or the MD or someone else within the firm instructed the receptionist to get three quotes for everything in future, which reduced his edge a little. Although even then, his long-standing contacts would give him an inside track on the price he had to beat, so he still kept the business more often than not.

However Peter made a very nice living out of being a genuinely nice, helpful person who focused serving his customers and made more than the running average out of simple print jobs that could, in all honesty, have been done cheaper by his competitors (albeit without the great service he also provided as standard).

So what's your equivalent of the undertaker, or my old colleague Peter? What do you buy which you'd never consider getting three quotes for...or alternatively what you haven't had three quotes for in quite some time?

Odds are there are easy pickings in there if you want to keep more of your cash in your own bank account instead of giving it to suppliers who've grown a little too comfortable.

Only rarely are these savings in the main things you buy for your business as most of those tend to be price-checked on a reasonably regular basis. But, like Peter with his letterheads, the greater source of cost savings in your business is often in the small but regular purchases of relatively unfashionable things, such as consumable items for the office or factory.

Anything you'd be reluctant to tender...for whatever reason...is almost certainly the place to start to find big cost savings and boost your cash flow.

Time investment: A few minutes per item to get some fresh prices from other suppliers.

Cash investment: Zero. For the sake of a short conversation or two, you can save substantial sums over the course of the year — a great return on your time investment.

Strategy 62 – What is your market?

I know you think you know what your market is but, in reality, few businesses think about what their market is in the best way possible.

The classic example is American railroads, all of whom had the opportunity to invest in new-fangled airlines and motor vehicles in the early years of the 20th century. All of them passed on the pitches they received, only to watch their long-haul passenger business disappear to the airlines and their short-haul passenger business disappear to cars and buses.

The US railroads thought they were in the railroad business. They forgot they were really in the "moving people around the country" business. If only they'd taken that perspective, perhaps some of the world's biggest airlines and automobile manufacturers today would be owned by the Union Pacific or the Burlington railroad companies.

More recently, Blockbuster Video, a name on every high street corner throughout the 1980s and 90s, was put out of business by the unstoppable rise of Netflix even though Blockbuster had the chance to buy Netflix (market cap at time of writing $120 billion) for just $50 million back in 2000.

The common problem — those businesses focused on themselves, not on their customers.

Early 20th century business travellers didn't want a train journey as such. They wanted to travel across the country as quickly as possible. It just so happened that, until airlines came along, trains were the best way to do that. As soon as there was a better way, the business travellers who dressed for dinner in the Pullman Car every night on their multi-day cross-country treks quickly disappeared.

In the 1980s and 90s, people just wanted to watch films at home. For as long as the only way to do that was jump in your car and drive to the video store to rent a film on video cassette for the night and return it to the same location the next day, that's what people did. As soon as a more convenient alternative came along...clicking a button on the remote control of your internet-enabled TV, for example...Blockbuster stores disappeared, never to return.

Similarly, the rise of Amazon put both corner bookstores and huge emporiums run by Barnes & Noble, Borders Books and Waterstones out to pasture.

The importance of these historical events in a book about cash flow is that you have opportunities to generate additional positive cash flow today...whether you realise it or not...by thinking about your services from the customer perspective and accommodating changing fashions in ways your product is consumed.

Every one of those previously all-powerful incumbents could have remodelled their business to ride the next wave of how people travelled across the country, or watched films at home, or bought books. And maybe in the very early days of all those new technologies there was a reason to be cautious about betting the farm on some new-fangled technology ultimately being successful.

But if you keep your focus on the problem your customer wants to solve, and not on your business as it operates within your existing industry structure, you'll find additional revenue opportunities even if that's just among the "early adopters".

If you keep your focus on your customer, as we cover in the Cash Flow Mastery programme, you'll build a business model that works best for you now...and adapts to customers' changing tastes and priorities in the future.

Keeping your focus on your customer minimises the chance of any competitors offering a completely different solution to your customers' problems won't nip in when you're not looking and pinch all your customers with their slicker, more convenient, more cost-effective service.

After all, if you don't have any customers, your cash flow isn't likely to look too pretty, no matter how long you've been in business or how closely you mirror your industry's current structure.

Time investment: You should already be spending time keeping up to date with your industry and your customers, so this will take no extra time beyond that.

Cash investment: In finding new ideas to deliver your products and services, little or none. To actually implement those solutions might require some investment, but if you're clear about your objectives and pursue a sensible plan to introduce new services and features while minimising cost and risk, any investment will quickly pay itself back and put you in positive cash flow territory.

Strategy 63 – What do people see when they first come across your firm?

One of the best ways to destroy your cashflow is to give people reason to doubt your firm is a professional, reputable business who will look after them properly. Anything you do to shake your customers' confidence will bounce back on you in ways you'll quickly regret.

I was thinking this earlier in the week when I was sat in a traffic jam behind a van belonging to a relatively well-known local business.

The branded vehicle left me in no doubt about whose van it was and how to contact them.

However, it also left me in no doubt about the fact that the rusting, dented, rather dirty vehicle was unlikely to belong to a company which took care of the details properly and would look after my business in a thorough and professional manner if I was to become one of their customers.

If they can't treat the simple matter of washing their vans properly and repairing any damage in a timely manner, I'm very unlikely to believe they're going to do anything else to a high standard.

It's an application of that old Van Halen thing where they had a standard rider in their performance contracts which demanded every venue place a large bowl of M&M's in the dressing room, but with all the brown ones removed.

Rather than being a sign of rock star excess, the band did this deliberately because if a concert promoter couldn't be trusted to do something as simple as that, they probably couldn't be trusted to have done anything else to the standard the band expected either.

When you're singing under lighting rigs weighing hundreds of pounds and plugging your instruments into dozens of different electrical sockets you hope are going to be safe, that "no brown M&M's" instruction isn't nearly as batty as it sounds.

I look for clues everywhere when I'm visiting a business for the first time.

Are there dirty coffee cups strewn around their reception area? Are the toilets clean and fresh? Am I greeted by a grunt a dishevelled, grumpy person when I walk in or greeted with a smile and a positive attitude so my first interaction with this business is a great one? These details matter.

Now, as it happens, I'm not in the market for the services of the firm who owned the van I was sat behind the other day, and I'm unlikely to need their services any time soon.

But rest assured as and when I might be in the market for the sort of services that firm provides, the only lasting impression I'll have of them is the dirty, rusting, ill-kempt van I spent 10 minutes sat behind in traffic the other day.

For a mission-critical service, I don't want to put my faith in a firm that can't work out a decent schedule for washing and repairing their own vans.

I'm unlikely to believe that a firm which evidently doesn't care much for its own property is going to somehow go the extra mile to care for mine if I give them my business. And I'm not alone in making judgements like that.

It costs little or nothing to present a professional image. It costs nothing to make sure dirty coffee cups aren't littering your reception area. It costs no more to have a smiling person on reception instead of a grumpy one.

So make sure you don't give potential customers reasons not to place their business with you, however trivial those reasons may seem. Otherwise you're not saving money...it's costing you a fortune.

Time investment: Little or nothing. Tidying things up, cleaning your vans and fixing things that are broken take almost no time to sort at all. And you don't even need to do it yourself, just make it clear to your staff what standards you expect and make sure they deliver on those standards.

Cash investment: Little or nothing beyond what you would have spent anyway. You've got to fix that van sooner or later, and it won't cost any more either way...if anything it will cost more the longer you leave it if rust takes hold in the meantime. So why not fix it now and present a professional image to your potential customers?

Strategy 64 – Will you still love me tomorrow?

"Will You Still Love Me Tomorrow" was a US Number One record for The Shirelles back in 1961.

And it's also a concept you can use to decide how important something is and whether you need to spend money on it.

I had a client once who was insistent that jobs which went into their factory were despatched on their transport that same day.

They quoted a seven-day lead time to their clients, but they'd put the job onto their production schedule the minute they had the information they needed from their client and an approved purchase order. And it would be on a trick that same night without fail. That was their Standard Operating Procedure.

The idea, in and of itself, wasn't a bad one. The intention was good and people on the shop floor had no doubt about what was expected from them.

Trouble is, that meant the job going out even if it took overtime in the factory to complete it, or required a later pickup, at a premium, from their courier company.

But their clients would still have "loved them tomorrow" even if they hadn't completed the job. After all, they still had several days left out of the seven they'd initially told the client.

Of course, I get all that "under-promise and over-deliver" stuff so beloved of simple-minded management consultants. And if you can do that at no extra cost, then overdeliver as much as you like as far as I'm concerned.

But don't let your own self-imposed ways of working increase your costs without good reason.

Putting on some overtime on day 7, if the job hadn't been done before then, would be a perfectly sensible strategy. But on day 3, against a 7-day delivery promise, you're just making life unnecessarily hard for yourself and increasing your costs for no great benefit.

Producing at the lowest-possible unit cost should always be your objective and that means, on occasion, sliding a little on the self-imposed rules you run your business by.

Yes, I know that makes things a little more complicated. And I acknowledge I spend a lot of time encouraging people to adopt and apply simple rules.

But if you enforce simple rules without the occasional exception...especially when that exception saves your business money...then you're being overly simplistic.

The objective for your factory management team shouldn't be "get every Job out the same day you start it".

The objective should be "produce work at the lowest possible unit cost, consistent with maintaining quality standards and meeting delivery promises to clients".

Sometimes that means not getting the job out. Especially when not doing so means your customer will still love you tomorrow.

Time investment: The extra time required to make a sensible decision over a less sensible one is next to nothing.

Cash investment: Zero. When you're producing at the lowest possible unit cost, consistent with maintaining quality standards and meeting delivery promises, you're saving money, not spending it.

Strategy 65 – Don't bury the lede

The lede is what journalists and copywriters call the opening few sentences in an article or some sales literature. (Pronounced as in the "lead" you'd use to walk a dog.)

There's a headline to attract your attention, then a few sentences to convey the most important points the writer wants to make and intrigue you enough to keep on reading the rest of the article. If those first few sentences don't want to make you read further, you won't.

Journalists and good marketers know if the most important information you want to convey isn't right up front to pull people in, a large proportion of readers will never know how important it was because they'll have stopped reading long before you get round to mentioning it.

A study by social media company Buffer showed that 55% of people decide if they're going to stop reading anything you put in front of them in 15 seconds or less. At an average reading speed of 200 words per minute, that means the majority of people won't read anything more than 50 words into your article, website post or marketing brochure.

At most, you've got a handful of sentences to make an impression or you'll lose your audience.

Why does this matter and how will it save you money?

Simple. You're conveying information to get people to do something you want all the time.

For a customer, you want to give them the information they're looking for, so they buy something from you. For an employee, that might be following the processes you designed to produce the right results for your clients at the lowest possible unit cost.

Anything that's not in your 50 words or so will be ignored by more than half of the people you put it in front of, if Buffer's research is anything to go by.

That new working procedure...the quote for some new business...the key information you want your bank manager to know...all of it needs to come up front, as if you were a journalist writing a story for their newspaper.

That gives clarity and saves wasted effort...and therefore cost. For all the things people should have done, but haven't because your communications weren't clear enough, it costs you more than it needs to because you've got to backtrack in order to get people back on the right path again.

It takes time you could have spent doing something much more productive, something that would take the business forward.

Not being clear about what you're proposing leads to people who might otherwise buy from your business going elsewhere...not necessarily in frustration, but certainly in confusion.

Just one word of warning. The most important piece of information for one of your customers isn't as you might think at first, the price of your product or service.

The most important information for your customer is how your business can solve a major problem they're currently grappling with. Unless you can be clear about that, whatever else you might say won't make any difference to them getting their chequebook out.

Interestingly, some online marketers, especially when talking to existing customers, slot a buy button immediately below the lede as well as in the more usual place near the end of a sales pitch.

What they've found is that a well-written lede makes their opening strong enough that a fair number of people won't even bother reading the rest of their sales proposal before they click that button to buy.

Every customer you can take from a state of confusion about what you're trying to tell them into a state of interest about how your unique solution solves a problem they're currently grappling with is more likely to buy what you're offering. That puts more money in your pocket and boosts your cash flow for virtually no extra effort. Just by thinking about how your business communicates.

Time investment: Little or nothing, as this is more about the presentation of something you'd be communicating anyway.

Cash investment: Zero. You're preparing the proposal anyway, so there are no costs beyond those you're already committed to, this is more about how you communicate that proposal to potential clients.

Strategy 66 – When did you last Google your business?

I once worked in a business where the Executive Team had successfully convinced themselves of their own genius. A point of view they persisted in believing even as everyone else working in the business could very clearly see it was headed down the toilet.

Each of the Exec Team had elaborate reasons for why they were doing a great job, presenting a comprehensive range of metrics to back up their claims, while gently hinting that any problems the business might be facing were due to another of their number not going a good enough job in their area of responsibility.

After a while, I got tired of this and did a "live" Google search on our company at one of our management meetings.

This threw up several issues and, let me warn you now, this is no way to win a popularity contest. But it did cut through the bluster in remarkably short order.

Firstly, despite the Marketing Director's frequent claims of how brilliant he was, this business — fairly prominent in its sector at the time — didn't appear until page 3 of Google when you searched for the products we sold within the geographical area we served. No matter how brilliant his branding and creative work might have been...something he had a range of awards and citations to "prove" ...it counted for nothing because virtually nobody in our target market ever saw it.

Something like 99% of Google searchers never click beyond page 1, so our marketing director was, at best, screaming into a blizzard.

The second issue this live search brought to the fore was that Google presents customer satisfaction reviews and ratings in its search results, often with direct quotes from places like Glassdoor and Trip Advisor if you search for the company name.

Despite the claims of the Director in charge of customer services that he was also brilliant, the public ratings were nothing short of embarrassing and some of the verbatim quotes right on the front page of Google when you searched for our business had everyone squirming in their seats.

As if that wasn't bad enough, the business was going through some tough times and had taken a number of deeply unpopular cost-cutting decisions which impacted on our workforce, who lived within the same communities as our target market. So, the search results were packed full of unflattering news stories about this business which also popped up automatically for anyone searching our company name on Google.

Putting ourselves in a potential customer's position, if we'd done a Google search on our business and somehow, despite the Marketing Director's best efforts, had actually found it...and then were immediately confronted with a series of cringeworthy direct quotes from desperately unhappy former employees and even more unhappy customers, combined with a blizzard of news stories telling the world what a hard time we were having, the likelihood is that none of us would be buying from this business either.

The tragedy is none of this was a secret. Except from the management team who were so convinced of their own brilliance they never looked at their business as a potential customer might. It didn't cost a penny to do the Google search — yet nobody ever had.

I won't pretend it was quick and easy, or indeed inexpensive, to put all this right. I left the business for greener pastures a few months later and most of the Exec Team were exited one way or another not long after I left.

But at least they now knew where to start if only they'd stepped outside their ivory tower for a moment. They didn't need a lot of fancy strategies, mission statements or values workshops, which is normally the sort of thing people do when faced with an underperforming business (and, believe me, we were no exception to that rule).

163

They could have saved tens of thousands of pounds in consulting fees and marketing expenses by just setting out to deal with the issues which had been in plain sight all along.

There's nothing more likely to scupper a sale, reduce your revenue and give you adverse cash flow than someone either not being able to find your business when searching online for the product or service you provide or, perhaps worse, finding it but at the same time coming across a slew of negative reviews and unflattering news stories.

Nobody in their right mind is going to buy from a business like that. And very few people did in this case either.

So, take a few minutes every so often to do a Google search on your own business. Whether you like the results or not, that's what the outside world sees when they go looking for your business. Through the Cash Flow Mastery programme we explore your business from an outside perspective — like it or not, that's how the world views your business, so we have to start from there. Details of Cash Flow Mastery follow at the end of the book.

If you'd think twice about buying from a business being roundly criticised, seemingly by everyone it interacted with, you can bet your bottom dollar plenty of other people will be do the same.

Finding out the problem brings issues of their own, because now you have to fix them, which may not be quick or easy. But at least it costs nothing to find out what the online world is saying about your business. And that alone could save you thousands.

Time investment: A few minutes every so often.

Cash investment: Zero.

Strategy 67 – Talking the customer's talk

A client showed me their new website recently, which was pretty darned good, I have to say. But there was one bit of it which used what I thought was slightly strange language to describe one of their services.

Whilst I could work out what the expression meant I knew this wasn't how they referred to this service within their business.

Aha, said the Managing Director, that's because our website people did some research and they found out that this is the most common search term people use when searching for those services. Although it's not how we talk about it, that's how our customers talk about it, so by talking about it in the same way on our website, we've seen a big increase in organic search traffic for that term.

Think about it.

My client didn't change their service in any way.

They would have had a page on their website to describe this service regardless, because it accounted for a significant part of their business.

Someone would have written the copy for that web page anyway, because they'd naturally want to talk about a service which brought in a decent income stream for the business on their new website.

So there was absolutely no extra cost in any of this for my client.

All they did, with the aid of a little bit of research, was describe the service in terms their potential customers would be searching for. Because they "talked their customer's talk", they naturally got a higher placing in the Google search results for this service.

That in turn meant they got more (free) organic search traffic so didn't need to advertise or promote this service as heavily as they might have done otherwise, which saved them money.

No other element in the process changed in the slightest, so there were no additional costs for my client. But "talking their customer's talk" lead to more business opportunities coming their way at a lower cost than they would have spent promoting their service with language their customers didn't use...which is what they'd been doing previously.

When you get potential customers delivered for free, instead of having to pay for the traffic to your website, that's got to be good news for your cash flow. Which, unsurprisingly, was true for my client too.

This is an exercise any business can benefit from, and it doesn't cost you a penny more than you would have spent anyway. A good marketer should be doing this sort of research as a matter of course, but some won't unless you ask the specific question.

With a few minutes to spare on Google, you can even do it yourself for free and pull in more customers for your business without spending a penny. That's got to be good for your cash flow.

Time investment: A few minutes a time for each of the products or services you offer.

Cash investment: Between zero (if you do it yourself) and not a lot (if your marketing agency does a quick bit of research for you).

Strategy 68 – Singing for your supper

Obviously, you need to be a decent singer to sing for your supper...unless your supper consists of food the audience throws at you.

However, it's much easier to speak for your lunch.

Business groups have a hard time finding people who will speak to a room-full of people at their meetings — anywhere from a dozen or so people, up to a hundred or more. And while I wouldn't recommend speaking to a room with a hundred people in it without getting some training and being pretty sure you're at least a halfway decent speaker, smaller audiences, especially those local to where you live, tend to be pretty forgiving.

There are three reasons for that. Firstly, those who have gone before you have generally set the bar pretty low. You don't need to be great to be at least no worse than them, and perhaps a little better.

Secondly, pretty much everyone in the audience is just glad they're not having to do the talk instead, so you benefit from their good wishes too.

And thirdly, most local businesspeople are interested in what other local businesses do, how they were started and how they grew into the business it is today.

So, seek out a local business group and offer to do a talk for them about your business or something you do...perhaps a pastime or hobby, even...which the local business community might be interested in.

And be creative with this. I do some speaking myself, but I rarely talk about accounting as very few people are interested in the nuts and bolts of accounting...even fellow accountants find this hard going.

However, every business is interested in how they can improve their profits, so that's what I talk about instead. Yes, this is just accounting under another guise, but it tends to go down much better with a business audience.

Cash Flow Surge

The great thing about being a speaker is that you're promoting your business to the audience (although you should try not to be too overtly promotional). Some of them will be prospects for your product or service, if not now, then at some point in the future. When that time comes, you'll stand out from your competitors who haven't done a talk to this business group, making it easier to close the sale when the opportunity to presents itself.

You also get some time to chat with members of the audience after your talk. Some of them will welcome a conversation about your products and services. And some of those will turn into customers without you having to compete against another provider or slash your prices to the bone.

You'll have done your business and personal credibility plenty of good by giving an interesting talk. And if that's all you get out of it, that's not a bad return for your time and effort.

But more likely than not, you'll get a customer out of it somewhere along the way. That customer will almost certainly be a lot easier to convert than someone who took a more conventional path through your marketing funnel. Odds are you'll get better prices from them too.

I know public speaking isn't for everyone, and there's that old stat about people being more afraid of public speaking than they are of dying, but it's not that hard. Certainly, if you've ever done a presentation to a customer, you're more than capable of doing a 20-minute talk to a lunchtime business group.

Buy a couple of books to help with the structure of your talk and make sure you practice a few times before you do it for real. but apart from that give it a go. Nobody is expecting you to out-do Tony Robbins, so don't even try.

Just be yourself and speak from your experience. And watch the interest from potential customers start to pile up at no cost to you, apart from a little bit of time.

Time investment: Obviously an hour or two to attend the event itself, and perhaps the same again to write your talk in the first place.

Cash investment: A maximum investment of a couple of books, which you can probably get second hand for pennies if you need to keep the cost down. And you save money on lunch too, as that will be paid for by the group you're speaking to, so you're probably cash-positive immediately!

Strategy 69 – It's not "first mover advantage" you want, it's second mover advantage

You hear a lot in the business press about "first mover advantage". This is the idea that the way to grow a big business is to pile in early and spend lots of money inventing your own technology and being prepared to lose money for years while you build up your customer base and develop a business worth billions of dollars.

Now, if you've got rich parents or a Silicon Valley venture capitalist has just given you billions of dollars which they can't take back again, then you might as well go for broke and do exactly that.

For the rest of us, though, broke is likely to be exactly where we'll end up pursuing this strategy.

The risk of failure is massive and explains why even businesses we're told to look up to today were not, by and large, first movers at all.

There were plenty of ways of playing music on a portable device before Apple invented the iPhone. There were social networks before Facebook — remember Friends Reunited? There was music sharing before Spotify, on services like Napster. There were places like MySpace to build an audience before YouTube. The list goes on.

If you have first mover advantage and through divine intervention or sheer dumb luck your business becomes a massive worldwide winner, there's no question you'll clean up financially.

But that outcome is so rare, you should exercise extreme caution in pursuing this path yourself. If good fortune is handed to you on a plate, then enjoy it. But don't be obsessed about achieving the supposed "first mover advantage" prize.

Most of the time, it's much better to be a second, or even a third or a fourth mover. Let someone else establish the market demand, go through the growing pains of trying to develop an idea into a marketable concept, finding people who can do something nobody else has done before.

Odds are they'll get some element of this wrong and you'll be able to come in on the back of that to create a more successful business of your own, having learned from the mistakes of others.

That's not just true for giant international businesses. It's true for local businesses in your own town too.

Has someone set up a business which is doing well, based on a good idea, but perhaps is pursuing a budget market when you could take essentially the same concept and offer an upmarket version of the same thing?

No matter how mundane you think your business is, there's a way to do that. When I was a kid, we put our dog into kennels when we went on holiday. You can still do that, but pet owners who want their pooches to be pampered while they're away can book them into "dog hotels" nowadays instead.

The result is the same, the dog gets looked after while their owners are away. But which one do you think gets to charge more to look after someone's pet? Same idea, two completely different price points.

Conversely, has someone got a great idea, but they're trying to sell it at a price very few people can afford? If you could somehow re-engineer that concept into a more affordable option, you might have a success on your hands.

Look at the idea of selling "time shares" on executive jets. Very few people have the tens of millions of dollars in free cash to buy an executive jet outright, but plenty of people who previously travelled business class or first class on conventional airlines could justify funding part-ownership of an executive jet from the savings in their valuable time, fewer overnight stays in hotels and faster point-to-point travel, meaning they could squeeze more activity into each day.

Maybe there's a struggling business, based on a sound-enough concept, but they've only half-solved the problem they were set up to deal with for their customers. Perhaps you could develop a successful business with a revamped product or service which covers off the elements the first business doesn't and sell your improved concept into that existing customer base.

There are so many reasons why, without rich parents or dumb investors, you should consider "second mover advantage" the best way to build your business. It's more likely to be successful, it's cheaper to create and it's less of a drain on your cash resources.

Making big bets on untested business models with your cash flow will only rarely...well into the tiny fractions of 1%...turn out to be good business decisions. I've seen plenty of businesses which went down that route and regretted it.

Those businesses were taken in by the nonsense you read in the business press about the big-name businesses whose founders bet everything they had to create a completely new market and somehow luck went in their favour, making them billionaires. (Although that's not normally how their stories are written up in the business press.)

If you want to keep more of your cash in your own bank account, don't fall for this.

Wait for second mover advantage to come around instead. You're much more likely to make your fortune that way, and until the opportunity comes along you can keep as much of your cash as possible in your own bank account.

Time investment: This saves you time because you're less likely to get sucked into blind alleys which will leech time, effort and financial resources away from your business without providing a return.

Cash investment: Zero. Not spending money on high-stakes gambles when the odds are strongly against you saves you money you could easily have wasted.

Strategy 70 – All hands on deck

If you've been in business for a while, you'll be familiar with everything taking twice as long as you think it should and the results only being half as good as you hoped.

That matters to your cash flow because it means you don't get as much done as you'd banked on, and whatever you do get, doesn't turn up until weeks, months or years after you really needed it.

But there's a simple way to turn that round, accelerate your cash flow and maximise the amount you've got coming in. It's a daily five minute "all hands" meeting.

After you've given people things to do, they'll get distracted. The siren call of their email inbox will cause them all kinds of trouble, not to mention the phone ringing and an array of day-to-day crises to sort out.

When you track back on why things haven't happened which you think should have happened, there's always a thousand reasons. And they're all legitimate in their own way. Your people aren't (usually) being lazy, they just get distracted by all the other important things going on in your business at the same time.

If you don't keep everyone focused on your biggest priorities the nature of modern business life means they'll drift away over time and spend their time on something else instead.

You can send people on all the time management courses in the world and spend thousands on HR visioning sessions, but it's all largely wasted effort...and certainly wasted money.

The only reliable way I've ever found to keep the focus of your team where it needs to be...on the activities you think are the most important...is to have a five minute catch up with your team every morning. If you work in a larger business you can do this as a cascade — you speak with your direct reports, then they do the same with theirs, and so on down the organisation right to the front line.

There are only two rules. Firstly, every member of the group has to be there because it's amazing how much impact even one person drifting in a different direction can have on the team as a whole. Secondly, it has to be literally five minutes.

If the daily meeting takes longer than five minutes you're either giving your team far too many different things to accomplish at the same time — in which case you might be better off thinking differently about how to set priorities better — or you haven't given them enough clarity about the task in hand, so you spend a lot of time going over strategies and ideas which should all have been sorted out long ago.

All that matters in your five-minute catch-up is what needs to happen today. The precise outcomes, the exact deliverables before everyone goes home tonight. It's a place for tasks to be allocated and prioritised, not for an ethereal discussion about business strategy.

If you do that every single day, you'll keep people on track and outcomes will get delivered faster and better, accelerating your cash flow and maximising your return on investment.

I know it's tempting to say, "I pay these people well and expect them to get on with things and not bother me with trivialities".

But, mostly, when people drift off a little as a result of spending some time in their email inbox or dealing with customer enquiries, they're trying to do what seems to them the right thing from the business's point of view, based on what they think your priorities might be. They're not setting out to undermine your potential.

Consider this. Most businesses say "customers are our first priority" in every strategy document and annual report. So, when a member of staff

175

has to choose between a project you've asked them to do and the phone ringing with a customer enquiry, which should they prioritise?

Well, if every strategy document and annual reports tells them "customers are our first priority", they're very likely to spend their time resolving the customer query instead of on whatever else you've asked them to do. Why wouldn't they? After all, customers being your first priority is what you tell them all the time.

That's just one small example, but often the reason for things not happening as quickly as you hoped isn't your staff being awkward, it's your staff trying their best to do what you've told them to do.

The good news is that you can put this right in five minutes a day.

When a staff member says they aren't making as much progress as they'd hoped on a project because they've been dealing with customer queries instead, this is your opportunity to demonstrate leadership.

Either reinforce that customers are indeed their priority or tell them to do their part of the project first because someone else is waiting for their work to be completed before they can move on to the nest stage of the project, and sort out the customer query later.

Doing otherwise is to abdicate your position as the leader, no matter what you think your team ought to be able to decide for themselves without your involvement. If they haven't decided for themselves already, or they've made the wrong call, that's on you to sort out — no-one else will.

If they're not working on your project, it's usually only because they're doing something else you've told them to do instead. The only person who can square that circle is you.

As you show that leadership over time, things get done faster, results get better and cash flow improves because your new ideas for the business get implemented sooner.

That five minute a day investment is one of the best investments you can make — it accelerates outcomes, improves results and costs you nothing.

Time investment: Five minutes a day...but strictly five minutes, no more!

Cash investment: Zero. You're already paying people to be there, so there's no extra cost, but there are big benefits from making faster decisions which lead to better outcomes and improved cash flow.

Strategy 71 – When you're better off not changing

A while ago I had a friend who had sweated buckets to design a new way of running as aspect of his business which reduced their costs and which, he thought, might be something they could sell to other businesses and open up a profitable new market for them.

As it happens, one of the target customer groups for this new venture were Finance Directors and Chief Financial Officers in medium sized businesses, so I asked my friend to pitch me with their "new, improved" offer as a relatively impartial source who represented the audience they wanted to reach.

He told me the changes they recommended would save me about 5% on the £10,000-20,000 a medium sized business was probably spending at the moment with their existing service provider.

Now, don't get me wrong, any Finance Director or CFO worth their salt is always interested in saving a bit of cash where they can. But this wasn't a terribly expensive service in the context of the other expenses in a business of this size. So, in effect, I was being asked to spend a couple of thousand pounds in up-front capital in return for savings of a few hundred pounds a year and a modest positive ROI over three to five years.

My friend ran a smallish business and the incumbent, in most cases, was a large, well-financed, "household name" business in the sector.

Any Finance Director and CFO worth their salt who faced that decision would, in addition to welcoming any cost savings, weigh up the additional risk of dealing with a small business who could disappear in a puff of smoke at any time, or who might deliver a poor service, leaving my business in the lurch.

This would make any Finance Director look like an idiot for leaving the comparative safety of a prominent multi-national to buy from an untested

SME trying to break into the market instead, on the slimmest of economic rationales.

I had to tell my friend...very gently... that the savings on offer just weren't enough, when set against the upfront investment and modest ongoing cost savings, to make me switch unless I'd already had some dealings with the business and been happy to use their services (in fairness, they were very good at what they did, but this was just a new venture for them where their previous track record wouldn't be all that relevant).

He was naturally a little disappointed, but I told him that the money he planned to spend building up this side of the business was unlikely to lead to the game-changing new income stream he hoped it would be...at least on its current economics.

More likely, the investment in the sales and marketing of this new idea would just saddle his business with a higher cost base than he had before without bringing in any extra revenue.

If you're doing something to attract new customers, especially when you're untested and untried in the market you're seeking to serve, the difference between whatever your target customers do now and what you'd like them to do in the future has to be dramatic, in terms of either cost or service. Then you might see the sales bump you were hoping for, with a surge in profits and positive cash flow to follow.

Half the price is dramatic. A 5% saving is interesting as far as it goes, but you're not going to get many switchers...and those you do get will be price shoppers who will go somewhere else the minute someone else offers them 5% off the price you're charging. There are some categories of customers you don't want to be encouraging, and price shoppers is one of them.

That's the importance of getting your business model right, something we cover in-depth as part of the Cash Flow Mastery programme (details at the end of the book). When the business model is out of kilter, you can easily throw fortunes at marketing a proposition which customers aren't interested in. Money you could have spent building your business in a different, more profitable, more cash-generative way instead.

I told my friend that if he wanted to grow his business, he might be better just investing his new product development budget on his existing products and services instead. After all they were a good business which gave a great service — they could grow that business quite nicely just by making sure more people knew they existed with very little investment and next to no risk.

Obviously, your mileage might vary, but don't assume that an idea which excites you because you've invested a lot of time, energy and mental effort in devising a solution will be received as enthusiastically by your customers as you perceive it yourself.

Before you start selling a new product or service, make sure you've considered what it might take to get potential customers to switch to you from their current service provider.

If you don't have a compelling business case, that's unlikely to generate increased positive cash flow...quite probably it will have the exact opposite effect.

Time investment: Nothing, apart from any time it takes to make sure you avoid being tempted by a slick presentation or an exciting new idea which doesn't add to your bottom line.

Cash investment: Zero. You save money by not doing something which won't add to your bottom line.

Strategy 72 – Principles vs tactics

Legendary advertising executive Bill Bernbach had a great saying – "Principles endure, formulas don't."

A lot of businesses I see don't spend enough time on the principles but spend far too much time on the tactics (or formulas, if you go back to Bill Bernbach's quote).

And that focus on formulas means you automatically increase the costs in your business.

There are two main reasons for that. Firstly, once you've "baked in" a formula, people tend to blindly follow it, irrespective of whether there's a better way of doing things. After all, nobody can be fired for doing exactly what you've told them to do.

Secondly, when a formula works less well that it used to, people tend to graft on another formula to supplement the one they have in place already. As you've already got people running formula 1, you'll naturally need to hire more people to operate formula 2 alongside formula 1.

That's bad enough, but the reality is new formulas are usually grafted on to a seething mass of other formulas which don't work anything like as well as they used to (if they ever did). The system has been tinkered with over the years and now resembles some Heath Robinson contraption instead of the slick business operation you'd hope to be running.

This in turn means each individual staff member is less efficient than they could be...and used to be... because the same hour of effort, on average, brings in less profit for your business than it used to when it's dissipated across a complex and slightly wobbly structure which doesn't fit together terribly well.

Try stepping aside from the overly restrictive approach of prescribing precise formulas, if for no other reason than "the right answer" for your customers will change over time.

One example I dealt with not long ago involved a client considering how best to get their products delivered to their customers the day after despatch from your factory, with 99%+ reliability.

Just in my working lifetime, I've come across several dozen ways to arrange a delivery to a client. I've even found businesses with three or four different ways of making a next day delivery depending on a bewildering array of factors, each of which took someone's time to calculate and implement.

But you can replace dozens of tactical formulas by telling the despatch department to choose the most cost-effective way of getting a parcel to your customers overnight, with a 99%+ reliability and then get out their way.

You've replaced a formula — possibly dozens of formulas —with a principle that anyone can understand. As long as the price is the lowest possible consistent with the service you promised your customer, what do you care if the service provider is Royal Mail or FedEx?

And since who you decide to send overnight parcels with is unlikely ever to be the biggest problem facing your business, you can spend your time much more productively on other activities which are more likely to move your business forward.

What's more, your despatch team won't need so much detailed monitoring and hand holding. With a simple principle in place, they can get on with the job they're hired to do with the minimum of supervision. This reduces both your operational and management costs, as well as freeing up everybody's time to focus on adding value to the business instead of policing the detailed application of a highly specific formula.

While this precise example might not be appropriate in the context of your business, as Bill Bernbach might have said, the principle of it certainly will be.

There are a small number of enduring principles every business needs to focus on, such as having a business model which generates a profit, collecting all the cash from customers as quickly as possible and ensuring high levels of customer satisfaction to maximise the chances of winning repeat business.

Get those principles right and the tactics, or formulas, largely work themselves out. That means your business costs less to operate because it's less complicated and less prone to error than building in a costly and inflexible infrastructure for management and oversight.

If there's one principle that's going to make it significantly easier to run your business efficiently and keep as much cash in your own bank account as possible, it's keeping things simple. Focus on the principles, let the formulas sort themselves out.

Time investment: This is a net time saving — expensive, senior people in many businesses spend way too much of their time on (relative) trivia. When your board is setting down procedures for which courier company to use, for example, that's unlikely to be a good use of their time. Keep the debate to principles and you'll save time and money which could be better spent elsewhere.

Cash investment: Zero. It's cheaper to run your business on principles, instead of tactics, so this saves you money in next to no time.

Strategy 73 – "I don't know"

It's tough being a business owner. As well as being a Finance Director and CFO, I've run businesses myself, so I know what it's like having everybody looking to you to make decisions all day long.

There have been times when I've spent all day answering questions for people and helping them to find the right answer to their problem before I even started work on what I was "supposed" to do.

Now, that doesn't mean my time was completely wasted. In some cases, it was a useful way to train a new member of staff or a way to do a bit of coaching with a longer-serving member of staff.

However, I had a coach called Tony for a while. He taught me the benefits of saying "I don't know...what do you think?" or "I'm not sure I've got a strong view one way or the other...how do you see the options?" whenever one of my team asked me a question.

The trick Tony taught me was to say that whether I already knew the answer or not.

The way he explained it made perfect sense.

When you make all the decisions, all you know is what you know. And nobody is smart enough to know everything — there's just too much information in the world for that to be a standard anyone can hope to live up to.

Asking someone else what they think can open up other ideas you might never have considered. Their perspective and experience will be different from yours, so let them take you through the options and make a recommendation rather than just immediately respond with your own perspective.

In reality, the majority of the time what your team member recommends will be exactly what you would have done anyway, but they benefit from going through the thinking process and will benefit from feeling that you have confidence in their judgement the next time they have a decision to make.

Occasionally, their recommendation will be something that doesn't make sense - perhaps they've overlooked some component of the decision in reaching their recommendation. That's your opportunity to gently mention the aspect they'd missed, or not considered in sufficient depth, and for them to learn for next time. As they hadn't implemented their initial recommendation, you've lost nothing and have helped someone improve for the future.

The rest of the time, you might just get an idea you wouldn't have considered and which represents a vastly better idea than the one you would probably have chosen if you'd just jumped in with your own answer when asked for your opinion. You might have missed out on an option which saves time and money, improves the service for your customers and boosts efficiency in your business.

Those decisions are a financial goldmine for your business and cost you nothing.

All it takes is 5-10 minutes of your time to let someone talk you through the options from their perspective and for you to coach them, if necessary, to making sure all the important factors are fully taken account of.

And, who knows, you might learn something in the process.

You might be the company's boss, but there's no need to be an all-seeing, all-knowing oracle.

Firstly that's a lot of pressure to place on yourself, but secondly people will have better ideas than you might have had, at least some of the time (and if you don't recognise the possibility of that, you've got bigger problems in your business than dealing with your cash flow, I assure you).

Every time you action an idea someone had which is better than your instinctive response would have been is an opportunity to save money and keep more cash in your business. It costs nothing to take Tony's advice from time to time and say, "I don't know...what do you think?"

Time investment: 5-10 minutes each time someone comes forward with a suggestion.

Cash investment: Zero beyond whatever you were going to spend anyway — and if the suggestion from your team member is better than what you'd have done, that means more cash coming into your business for no extra cost.

Strategy 74 – Is your business in the twilight zone?

The Twilight Zone was an old TV programme about spooky goings-on and unexpected events.

But every business is chock-full of spooky goings-on and unexpected events.

All those things you thought were taken care of, but which came back to bite you. All the instructions you gave that never seemed to be actioned in practice. All the objectives agreed in your team's performance reviews which weren't completed by the allotted time.

If you're like most business owners, this causes some significant degree of frustration. After all, how hard can it be?

Well, the problem is in the Twilight Zone where spooky things happen.

Except they're not that spooky...

The problem is you've only been thinking in one dimension. You give an instruction, someone carries it out. That's just one dimension to worry about and if you're dealing with an engineering or science problem, that might be all you need to do.

Add one unit of oxygen to two units of hydrogen and you get water absolutely 100% of the time. It's one of the inviolable rules of the physical universe.

Almost nothing in business works like this. Every time humans are involved, there are multiple dimensions to take into account.

Perhaps the person you've given instructions to doesn't work directly for you — when they get back to their normal department, their line manager gives them something else to do and tells them that should take priority. Your junior employee is likely to do what their line manager tells them as they control the salary increases and performance reviews for their department.

And your manager is only likely to prioritise something else because you've told them it's got to take priority. They're only doing their best to carry out your instructions, as best they understand them.

And that's just two dimensions. Factor in the reaction from customers, the perspectives of regulatory bodies, the opinions of investors and complexity quickly bubbles out of control.

When complexity starts bubbling out of control, most businesses build in extra costs to try to manage the complexity out again. Yes, it costs you money to combat the gravitational pull of the twilight zone, where good ideas go do be forgotten.

The way to combat this is by keeping your operations simple.

Steve Jobs, co-founder of Apple, wisely said "Simple can be harder than complex. You have to work hard to get your thinking clean to make it simple. But it's worth it in the end because, when you get there, you can move mountains."

His philosophy took Apple from a garage-based start-up to the world's most valuable company in just a few decades.

The lowest cost way of doing anything...the quickest way of getting anywhere...is the simplest way possible. That's why simplifying your operations is a key part of our Cash Flow Mastery programme, details of which can be found at the end of this book.

The more you complicate things, the more "twilight zone" opportunities you build into your business, the more places good ideas have to go to be forgotten. And the higher price you need to pay to keep things on track by regularly dragging your ideas clear of the powerful gravitational pull of the twilight zone.

Cut out the distractions and you cut out the cost. So, making things simple is usually the lowest cost way to keep your cash flow strong, with the least amount of effort on your part.

Time investment: Simple can be hard up-front, but it takes much less time to keep the show on the road afterwards, meaning you quickly come out ahead.

Cash investment: Little or nothing — thinking doesn't cost more in any business. The brains are already there, you just need to get them focused on the right problems.

Strategy 75 – Sorry isn't the hardest word, communication is

Nielsen is a company which, amongst other things, is used by US advertisers to track viewership of TV programmes, which in turn determines how much the advertiser will pay for a 30-second commercial in the middle of a popular TV show.

A couple of years ago Nielsen did some research into how memorable TV commercials are...bear in mind these tend to be for large brands with big budgets who spend a fortune trying to get you to remember their name and their product. No psychological technique is spared trying to get their message across.

Nielsen tested viewers' ability to recall ads a few minutes after seeing 49 separate messages which, as you can imagine, was pretty good.

But here's the kicker. Just 24 hours later...a single day after seeing the commercial...viewers' ability to recall those same ads was down by 50%. Half the people couldn't remember something they'd seen just the day beforehand.

US TV viewers are not uniquely stupid. We all have busy lives and anything we don't immediately need has a lot of trouble staying in the forefront of our minds. We've got the kids to pick up, that report to do for the boss before 9am tomorrow, the ingredients we need to buy for dinner tonight and all the other things that go in inside our heads.

It's also depends on the context.

If you're in the market for a new car, you'd probably remember a string of different car commercials. But if you don't plan on changing your car for another three or four years, the likelihood is you'll tune all the car commercials out altogether because they just don't matter enough for you to keep the details in the precious memory space where there's already got more than enough going on.

It's the same way with communication inside your business. It's tempting to think that because you're the boss and you've handed down your words on tablets of stone things will just happen. But a day later, something else will have come along for people to think about instead, meaning whatever you said yesterday will have been put firmly on the back burner.

At the same time, the reason you're communicating is to improve something in your business – make more sales, reduce costs, identify opportunities or whatever the case might be. So, for as long as your message gets treated like the a car commercial your staff sees when they're not in the market for a new car, your business won't see the benefits in profits and cash flow you might have hoped for either.

There's a real art to good communication.

And it's more than just repeating the same message over and over. That just becomes like your mum nagging you to tidy up your bedroom when you were a teenager…most teenagers, and indeed most parents, know how well that usually turns out.

You've got to try different messages, variations on a theme, different people being involved and putting their own spin on a principle you've espoused.

You've got to recognise people who do what you ask, quickly and professionally.

And before you say, "isn't that what I'm already paying them for?", that might be true, but since most people don't even do that, give those who follow through some recognition anyway to encourage the others to do the same.

Communicating well is hard, which is why it's so rare. But you don't need to be perfect, you just need to be better than most other people and you'll still dominate your industry and run a high-performing business.

Since most of us aren't taught to communicate, take a class, book onto a course, hire a coach who specialises in communication so you can learn from people who know how to communicate well. It might cost you a few hundred pounds, but you're unlikely to get a better return on investment than from spending a little bit of time and money learning to communicate better.

In most businesses, very few people remember what they've been told. If you could get twice as many of your staff remembering what you've said, even just 24 hours after you said it, and taking action as a consequence, your business would be streets ahead of your competitors in no time.

Time investment: A few hours over the course of a few months.

Cash investment: Somewhere between nothing and a few hundred pounds, depending on how you plan to improve your communication skills. But it's money well spent as your business will grow profits by many multiples of whatever it cost you within a few weeks, so don't let a small initial investment put you off.

Strategy 76 – The Pepsi Challenge

In 2018, Pepsi spent $4.2 billion on marketing. That's quite a chunk of change, although not quite as much as Coca Cola who spent $5.8 billion in the same period.

One way or another, a lot of that ad spend is trying to create a distinction between the two products in a customer's mind, when the truth is there's very little difference. Both are brown, fizzy liquids, generally sold cold, both of which give a simultaneous rush of sugar and caffeine that will pretty much guarantee you'll want another one in a couple of hours when the effects start to wear off.

I know everyone has their preference...but think about it. Have you ever walked out of a bar or a restaurant when you've said, "can I have a Coke, please?" and they respond with "is Pepsi OK?" (or indeed the other way around).

Certainly, I've never walked out of somewhere just because they didn't have the particular brown fizzy liquid I asked for, and I don't know anyone who ever has. Most people just aren't as bothered as the soft drinks companies hoped we might be when they sanctioned spending $10 billion a year on marketing between them.

Trying to convince customers there's a big difference between two brands which customers see as more or less identical is an expensive business. If $10 billion isn't enough, then whatever your marketing budget might be probably isn't either.

Although they probably wouldn't admit it publicly, Coke and Pepsi realise that and have put a lot of effort in recent years into getting shelf space and product availability. If the Coke is in a fridge, I'd probably buy that over an unrefrigerated Pepsi on a shelf. Equally, I'd buy a Pepsi if that brand was the cold one.

Or if I've rushed into a shop for a quick drink between meetings and the Pepsi fridge is at the front of the shop near where I came in, and the generic fridge with the Coke and a range of other soft drinks in it is stuck away at the back, I'm unlikely to walk to the rear of the shop. Ditto if the roles were reversed.

What's that got to do with your cash flow?

Simple. It's all about spending your money wisely.

Either Coke or Pepsi could probably save a couple of billion dollars from their marketing budget and not notice the difference. Nobody probably objects to their ads, but they're clearly not driving purchasing decisions to any great extent.

But if they spent a couple of billion dollars less on fridges, or product placement next to the tills, or whatever, they'd both notice the difference by the end of week 1.

Of course, you want to grow your business, and that takes some investment in marketing. The trick is to know which sort of marketing needs doing.

TV ads, cinema ads, shirt sponsorship for Premier League football teams and the like are all expensive ways to promote your business. And in the case of Coke and Pepsi, that investment would seem to be largely wasted as very few people are passionate enough buyers to insist on their favourite brand or to make a scene if they don't get it.

A handful of branded fridges, by comparison, cost very little and stay in place for a long time with almost no effort on their part.

If you're investing heavily to grow your business, invest in the things that make a difference to people's likelihood to buy from you, not things which might be fun or cool or win awards for the marketing agency.

Remember "Lip-smacking, thirst-quenching, etc, etc" Pepsi? Or Coke wanting to teach the world to sing (in perfect harmony)? Or the Pepsi Challenge, where Pepsi got consumers to do a blind taste test to find which brand they preferred (surprise, surprise, it was usually Pepsi)?

Billions of dollars later, still nobody knows the difference or even cares very much.

Spend some time working out the real drivers behind customers buying your product instead of just throwing money at your advertising budget — and, a word of warning here, it's never what customers say it is, watch what they actually do instead and build your plan around that — then go all-in on whatever sparks their purchasing decision.

If you were running a brown, fizzy water business, you might save fortunes if, instead of running your award-winning advertising, you invested all your cash in putting branded fridges next to the tills in every shop you could find instead.

Find out what the equivalent is in your business, and you can save a fortune compared to all your competitors and still beat them in the fight for the contents of your customers' wallets.

Time investment: Very little — by the time you notice different customers doing the same thing half a dozen times in succession, that's probably the feature to concentrate on.

Cash investment: Zero. At first just carve out a small share of your existing marketing spend until you've proved the concept works. Once you're up and running, you can cut your marketing costs overall, even as you watch your sales grow, because you'll be spending your budget much more wisely than your competitors.

Strategy 77 – Everybody wants choice, but who's prepared to pay for it?

We've all heard the story about Henry Ford telling the customer who asked if they could choose the colour on their Model T "you can have any colour you like as long as it's black".

There's a fine dividing line here. Naturally you want your customers to buy from you rather than anybody else so if someone wants their car in green instead of black, you'd probably try to get it in that colour for them. Or if they want your product in a larger size. Or a smaller size.

In fact, you should offer some options for your products, as outlined in one of our earlier strategies, as that will bring in more sales than just offering one choice. And that's true pretty much no matter what you sell.

But there's also a point at which you should stop being so accommodating and should make a firm decision not to offer any more options. And the reason is the cost — not just the cost of materials, but the cost of stockholding, warehousing, needing extra pages on your website to accommodate the variations, needing to have staff with varying levels of expertise on hand to cater for every eventuality, and so on. That can get expensive.

The cost is always more than you think it is. One business I know thinks its variations don't cost them anything as they make an additional charge for the artwork if they reproduce it on a different sized product.

Except the charge they make for their artwork on different sized products is relatively modest, just the few pounds in studio time it takes to amend the original image held on file.

They haven't priced in the need to run two different order systems, the extra stockholding costs for different sized raw materials, the number of times they don't have size 1 in stock but offer size 2 at the same price to keep the customer happy, the changeover time in their production processes to go from size 1 to size 2, and so on.

Variations always cost a lot more than businesses think they do.

So much so, if they factored in the real, full cost very few people would pay the extra charges involved ("but it's just a couple of lines of text different!").

Henry Ford's approach, with one single option, is far too restrictive in today's world. In fact, it was far too restrictive even for Henry Ford 100 years ago because General Motors won business away from Ford at least in part on the strength of them being able to offer colour options other than black.

And some options are good. If you don't have any at present, there's a strong argument for up to three options as we talk about elsewhere in this book (assuming you get the pricing right to make sure the variations add to your bottom line).

But beyond that, options and variation cost money and it's usually money you can't, or won't, charge in full to your customer. You end up swallowing a lot of the extra costs one way or the other.

The customer isn't always right. If you're offering a reasonable range of options, you're under no obligation to do everything your customer wants. If your quality, service and pricing is high, people will still buy from you even though you don't offer, say, a pink Model T Ford as standard.

Anyone who's keen enough on a particular colour choice can take it to a third-party paint shop to get it any colour they want. You might even give customers a list of some such places with every black model T sold.

That costs you nothing, and you same a lot of money by helping customers get the solution they want without having to re-set your machines for every random customer request that comes along.

Time investment: Little or nothing — beyond a sensible range of options you're nearly always safer saying "no" unless someone's giving you a blank cheque for whatever the costs might turn out to be when you've tracked the real extra costs of producing the job through your business.

Cash investment: Zero. You're saving money, not spending it.

Strategy 78 – Lemon

"Lemon" is the headline on a classic mid-1960s Volkswagen ad in the US.

It's not a term we really use in the UK, but in this context a "lemon" was a slang term used to describe a car that started breaking down the minute you got it out the showroom, almost immediately after the dealer had cashed your cheque.

Photographing your product next to the word "lemon" and running full-page newspaper ads on that basis was a bold move for DDB, Volkswagen's agency.

When you read the little bit of copy at the bottom of the page, the story was very different from the first impression. It illustrated that VW's standards were so high they'd send a car back to get put right even if it was for a minor flaw most of their competitors would have allowed to go through to the end-customer.

And there's something quite neat in this. Once you get a reputation for being utterly reliable you can charge premium prices and attract a loyal customer base who value dependability highly.

Of course, you'll miss out on some price shoppers, but that may be no bad thing as they'll be heading for the hills as soon as someone else shaves a few pennies off your prices anyway. But you'll attract a lot more customers than you lose, over time, and with relatively little marketing effort.

In the Volkswagen "Lemon" ads, they made a fuss about the chrome strip on the glove compartment being slightly blemished... "Chances are you wouldn't have noticed. Inspector Kurt Kroner did." They go on to say they reject one car out of 50 for failing one of the 189 checks they carry out before a VW Beetle leaves the factory.

The brilliance of the Lemon ads is that by admitting a flaw and demonstrating what they do to put it right again, we trust the business more. After all, if we had noticed that slightly blemished chrome slip on the glove compartment, we might have wondered what else hadn't been checked properly on the car before it was allowed to leave the factory.

You can't put a price on your customers' trust. Yes, VW could have let your VW Beetle through and saved a few quid replacing the chrome strip on the glove compartment - or whatever the equivalent might be in your business. But it's false economy. Eventually customers trust your business less and so reduce the amount they're prepared to pay for your products or services as they feel they need to keep something in reserve in case they need to fix something you've missed.

With a reputation for un-matched quality and an attention to detail which borders on the obsessive (the VW ads pointed out they employed more quality inspectors than the number of cars they produced each day) sales are easier to come by, customers are happier and you benefit from their recommendations to friends and family.

More recently Lexus built a major luxury car brand from nothing by doing something very similar. I know several Lexus owners with their own stories of obsessive customer service and unbeatable quality, which they tell people they come across on a regular basis.

So, admitting your flaws can be good for business. It helps people see how committed you are to the very highest standards of quality and service. The more you make a fuss of it, the more this becomes a key part of your marketing message, the more people buy, the more they recommend you to their family and friends.

That's the sort of virtuous cycle you'll learn how to build in our Cash Flow Mastery programme, and it's a great way to build a business with little or no upfront investment in time or money.

Admit your flaws...and demonstrate what you do to put them right. Then watch the sales flow and the profits follow. That puts a lot more cash in your bank account than letting something through which isn't quite right and hoping your customer won't notice.

Time investment: Little or nothing. This is just doing the job right, which is what should have happened in the first place anyway.

Cash investment: For some things it can require a small amount of cash, relative to the sales value of your product or service, to put things right. But you'll get the difference back many-fold once word gets around that you're the place to go when you want a quality job doing.

Strategy 79 – Better isn't necessarily best

We live in a world obsessed with innovation. Digital technologies promise to do all sorts of clever things our parents and grandparents can only marvel at. Seemingly every day, some tech company or other launches an app that's going to change the world (or so they claim…).

There's always an argument for moving forward, investing in new technology, boldly going where nobody's gone before.

But sometimes, at least, those arguments don't stand up to analysis.

The best example I know is the tale of the sinking of the Bismarck in World War Two. The Bismarck was the mightiest ship ever to take to the high seas at the time. It was fearsomely fast, well-armed and, unusually for a battleship at the time, didn't travel with a flotilla of escort ships because it was so fast and manoeuvrable the escorts would only slow it down.

There was no more modern, better designed, better armed ship afloat. It was the poster boy for elegant naval design and had the firepower to ward off any potential enemy ship all by itself.

The Bismarck was a technological marvel for its day.

Yet it was ruthlessly destroyed by a bunch of obsolete biplanes.

You see, the Bismarck was perfectly prepared for an attack from the fast, high-flying aeroplanes of the day – the Spitfires and Hurricanes, the Lancasters and the fighter-bombers. The radar-controlled gun turrets on the Bismarck were set up for that sort of air attack.

What they weren't prepared for was an attack from a squadron of Swordfish — a rickety old biplane from the early 1930s, armed with a single torpedo.

These planes were incredibly slow, flying at just 90mph compared to around 350mph for a Spitfire. The crew of three sat in an open cockpit. The

Swordfish were nicknamed "stringbags" because that's what the myriad of wires and struts holding the wings together made them look like. This was not the glamorous end of the aviation industry.

Yet they did what others couldn't. The came in low, just above the white caps on the waves, hard to track and hard to shoot down with the ship's anti-aircraft guns. And ponderously slow.

Despite all the disadvantages of the Swordfish, their torpedoes disabled the most powerful naval vessel of its time, which was eventually scuttled by its crew.

At the time, you couldn't have got better than the Bismarck. But the Bismarck wasn't the best.

It came off second best to a squadron of museum pieces.

And in the world of business this happens all the time. It's really tempting to invest in the new cutting-edge solution to something, but not all those solutions work as well as people claim, and some don't even work at all.

That's because sometimes we forget the lesson of the Swordfish. It's the results which determine whether something is a success or not.

You'll be glad to know that inside Cash Flow Mastery, we focus on results that work, like the Swordfish, not necessarily results that just look pretty, like the Bismark. More information on this programme at the end of this book.

You see, it isn't how pretty it is or how elegant it is or how well-conceived something is. If success was determined by any of those qualities, the Bismarck would have won hands-down.

But in business, as in war, that's not the measure. Just looking pretty doesn't win any battles. Being effective is all that counts.

So, before you invest in new technology, make sure it's going to be a lot more effective than what you do now. Not just a little bit more effective, but a lot more effective. Twice as effective, not 10% more effective.

If gains are only marginal, you're almost certainly better off doing nothing. Investment will only increase your fixed costs and the benefits you get won't be enough to offset the increase in your cost base. You'll actually be worse off, not better off, when it comes to the state of your bank account.

Don't be taken in by bright shiny things. They could just be the Bismarck in disguise.

And if it is, you might be better off sticking with a Swordfish.

Time investment: This saves you time you might have spent on the latest ideas which don't deliver on their promise.

Cash investment: If there's no investment to make, you're not spending any cash. This keeps more money in your own bank account to use as you please, instead of handing it over to someone who promises the earth but doesn't deliver.

Strategy 80 – Scepticism vs cynicism

In business, you have to be mildly disbelieving of everything people tell you.

Your own staff will want to present the most positive view possible of their own performance.

Your suppliers will want to promise you that everything will be just fine, even though they know it might not be.

Your customers will promise to be fair and reasonable, but some of them will be anything but (pro tip: they're usually the customers who spend a lot of time upfront telling you how fair and reasonable they are going to be...).

So, a degree of scepticism isn't a bad thing. In fact, it's a vital survival tactic if you plan on being in business for the long term.

But don't over-do it and become cynical.

Scepticism is being unwilling to change your mind until someone proves you wrong.

Cynicism is refusing to change your mind even after someone has proved you wrong.

And that never ends well.

The trouble is, in the end, if you refuse to change your views in the face of overwhelming evidence which contradicts your beliefs, the brutal combination of harsh reality and the laws of fundamental economics will always catch you out...often sooner than you think.

Yes, if you're determined enough you can sometimes postpone the day of reckoning a little. But when reality strikes it can dismantle someone's business like a tsunami hitting the coast of a low-lying Pacific island.

The most extreme case I encountered was a CEO who'd set a £4million sales target for one of the divisions of the business and kept insisting that was still going to get delivered even though by Month 10 they hadn't yet reached £1million in revenues for the year so far.

What's more, looking at the sales pipeline for the following two months, there was probably only another £2-300,000, at best, of income still to come. We also knew all our competitors were struggling for sales volume too.

And this was in a "long cycle" business — you could see new business coming several months in advance and there just wasn't enough in the pipeline to magically put all this right in the 60 days left in that financial year, especially with so many of our competitors scrapping with us over what little business there was.

The CEO refused to believe the evidence in front of their own eyes. They were too wrapped up in their own view of the world to consider for a moment that their plans had gone badly off course and too invested in their self-image to be prepared to admit they'd got it wrong.

Needless to say, the business hit the rocks pretty hard shortly thereafter and the CEO was quickly turfed out, forever to be remembered within the business as a delusional fool who refused to see what every other single member of staff could.

How this impacts your cash flow is that the CEO spent like a sailor on everything they could think of to boost the income in this division. They took on high-priced salespeople, invested in marketing, ramped up the cost base to, in their words, "attract more customers".

None of those strategies were in themselves completely off-base, given enough time.

But given the sales cycle in this business, none of those strategies would have had an impact by the end of the financial year when they needed to have booked the sales to fix the hole they'd created in the year-end balance sheet.

The CEO would have been better off re-grouping, reducing costs selectively, and seeking to build through to the following year when the business might well have made it through with only minor bruising to the CEO's ego.

Refusing to even consider the evidence placed in front of them because it didn't fit their own view of the world led to this CEO's downfall. The price of not delivering was much greater than the price of admitting they were not going to realise £4m in sales for this division until the following financial year.

By all means by sceptical in your business. You probably aren't getting the full picture right off the bat. You should push for evidence as much as possible.

But when you get that evidence, and you're satisfied as to its quality and probity, you need to take that on board even if it doesn't fit the narrative you've constructed for yourself.

Reality matters a lot more than anything else. You bank and investors will be happy for you to believe anything you like as long as the reality they see is that you deliver what you promised.

If you don't, you can believe anything you like, but it won't matter. The banks and investors will take you out, no matter what stories you tell yourself. All they're bothered about is reality.

Time investment: Little or nothing. Just check yourself from time to time and ask if you're being sceptical or cynical when a subordinate tells you something you don't like the sound of.

Cash investment: Zero. It's always cheaper to be guided by reality, not suckered in by vanity.

Strategy 81 – Run with spare capacity

Earlier today I saw a TV news story about a lady who needed a special sort of medical food supply, but the government had shut down the only place it was produced in the UK following an inspection of some sort.

This unfortunate lady had gone 10 days without eating because her body was incapable of digesting the sort of food most of us eat as a matter of course following an operation which had left only 20cm of her intestines intact.

Now, I know we're talking about the government here so, by definition, most of their decisions are indescribably stupid. But this takes "indescribably stupid" to a whole new level.

In the entire United Kingdom, there was only one factory which produced the special food which is the only nourishment this lady, and a certain group of people with the same medical condition, can consume to stay alive. Without this food literally starve to death.

The geniuses in Whitehall thought it made sense to have a single source of supply for this...no doubt on the basis that it was cheaper per unit to put everything through the one contract. At no point, it would seem, did they consider the risks of this factory not being able to produce, for whatever reason, nor did they have a backup plan in place (or if they did, it wasn't a very good one).

Thankfully, this lady got a fresh food supply 10 days into the crisis. But coming that close to certain death just because some civil servant had only considered the cost of production, and hadn't factored in what might need to happen in the event things went wrong at the factory, would make me particularly twitchy about my odds of surviving into old age.

Hopefully you'll never find yourself in a position like this, but it highlights something I always say to clients.

The most expensive things you'll buy are the things you need in a desperate hurry. That's why you should always run with some spare capacity in your business.

I know Finance Directors and CFOs are normally keen on "sweating the assets", that is keeping everything possible operating the maximum number of hours.

That's not completely unreasonable. The most basic financial modelling tells you the same costs spread across 24 hours a day will be much less per unit than if they were spread across just 8 hours a day.

But what happens if you fill up your productive capacity 24 hours a day and the machine breaks?

I've seen businesses suffer financial penalties for not delivering products on the contractual delivery schedule because they'd filled up their production 24 hours a day 7 days a week and then experienced problems with their machines which prevented on-time despatch.

I know it's tempting to say, "we'll cross that bridge if we come to it" or "having all our machines full sounds like a nice problem to have".

Trouble is, when you've filled up every ounce of productive capacity — whether that's your machines or your people — you've got nowhere to go.

Putting the situation right will be expensive. That might mean contractual penalties for late delivery. Or overtime costs for your staff. Or premium-rate repairs to a machine because you can't afford to let the machine stand idle any longer than absolutely necessary.

The list goes on, but the key takeaway is this. If you fill up every ounce of productive capacity and something goes wrong, everything you do from that point onwards is going to cost you money. A lot more than it would have cost to run with some spare capacity in the first place.

It's classic "penny-wise, pound-foolish" behaviour that costs your business real hard cash to put right, and your negotiating position with your staff and suppliers will be somewhere between weak and non-existent when your back is against the wall. They'll make hay while the sun shines and you won't have any options.

This might sound like an argument for spending more than you have to which, you might think, is the exact opposite of what this book is supposed to be about.

But a long career in a variety of businesses has taught me that the lowest cost way to run a business isn't to fill up all your productive capacity. That's the sort of important subtlety you'll pick up inside our Cash Flow Mastery programme — full details of how that works at the end of this book.

You need to run with some headroom, and have options for how you'd still get the work out if machine A broke down suddenly — can you put the work on machine B instead...could you work overtime on the rest of your machines to get this week's jobs out on schedule even without machine A in production...could you rent a piece of equipment to keep going somehow, even if not quite so efficiently, until your machine was back up and running again?

When you've got spare capacity, that means you aren't paying penalties to customers, you aren't paying overtime to your workforce, you aren't getting charged premium rates by your suppliers for fixing things in a hurry, and so on.

Sometimes the best way to save money and boost your cash flow is not to fill up every moment of your productive capacity, whether that's your people or your machines.

Time investment: Little or none. Just resist the temptation to over-fill your factory or your people.

Cash investment: Zero, in the sense that you've already bought the machines and employed the people. This is about how you can still make things work with the equipment and people you've got, even if a paper exercise might suggest that you could get by without one of your machines. More often than you might think, getting rid of productive capacity will come back to bite you, and that's when your costs skyrocket by a lot more than whatever you save in the short-term.

Strategy 82 – "What have I done for these people lately?"

Try this exercise — take a sheet of paper and split it into three sections running down the page.

Write down the names of the 10 people you know within your existing business connections who could do the most to propel your business forward. Not your wish list of "wouldn't it be great to meet Richard Branson or Elon Musk one day", but people from your current business connections – people you've met in person or connected with on LinkedIn or have their business card in a box in your drawer.

List them down the page in a single column. Don't worry too much about the order, and if the number turns out to be 11 or 12, that's not the end of the world.

If there's only three of four people in your existing connections who can propel your business forward, you've got an entirely different problem, which we'll get to later. But most people find it harder to cut down to 10 than to build up to 10, so let's assume that's the camp you're in too.

Once you've got your list of the 10 people among your current business connections who can do the most to propel your business forward, go back to the top of your list. Then go down the list again and in the next column write against each name what the last thing you did for them was.

Finally, in the third column write down approximately when that was – you don't need to have this down to the precise date. Earlier this week or last month or last summer is just fine.

If you're like most people, you'll be surprised how hard it is to remember when you last did something for them.

I'm not talking about the fact you delivered their order on time earlier this week, or some such activity, however laudable that might have been.

This is about what you've done to help them personally or professionally over and above what you would have done anyway as part of your normal course of business.

But hang on, you might say, we've done the job we were asked to. Isn't that enough?

Well for servicing your client and keeping your nose clean it probably is. But is it enough to make sure you keep the business with this client if someone is pitching against you? On its own, probably not.

Is it enough that you can call your connection, ask them to do you a monumental favour which would catapult your business into the next league and be confident they'd do whatever you asked in a heartbeat? Probably not.

And if whatever you wrote down on that sheet of paper isn't enough to spark that reaction, you've got untapped potential to grow your business at little or no cost.

In general, people don't want to be flown on a private jet to watch the Monaco Grand Prix (although they're unlikely to turn an offer like that down). They want to look good in front of their boss. They want you to introduce them to your brother who works at a firm they'd like to have as clients. They want you to mention to them that there's a great job opening you've heard about which would be a great promotion opportunity for them.

None of those cost you a penny, beyond the cost of a phone call.

Do any one of those things and what is your customer likely to do next time one of your competitors comes to call? They'll listen politely, but you'll keep the business.

More than that, when you've found them a juicy new job, might they make an introduction to one of their friends who would be a perfect customer for you? You bet — most of us would want to return the favour.

213

The key here is that they're "returning" the favour. You need to **do** the favour first before it can be returned.

Most of us don't do enough to build our relationships with people who might be able to help before we ask for a favour. So, surprise surprise, we often get rebuffed — if not directly, at least indirectly. An unenthusiastic lukewarm introduction to someone can be worse than no introduction at all.

Take a look at that list of 10 names again.

If it's a while since you did them a favour, what can you do to make something happen today? If you're never done them a favour...a surprisingly common reaction when I ask people to do this exercise...now might be a good time to start.

Pro tip: don't go all starry-eyed because you're dealing with someone you think is more important than you, so they don't need your help. Everyone always needs more help in their life, no matter who they are and what they have that you don't.

In a funny way, important people have fewer people doing them favours because everyone presumes they don't need any help. You actually stand out more.

When you help other people, no matter how lowly or highly they rank on an organisation chart somewhere, you're helping the world go around. Of course, some people will take advantage, but most won't. Most will be glad to return the favour.

You benefit short-term by protecting the business you already have. You benefit long-term by taking your business in directions you couldn't begin to imagine. And you do it all at little or no cost.

If it's a while since you helped someone who's important to your business, today might be a good day to start.

Time investment: A few minutes here and there to make an occasional phone call or ask a friend of family member if you can introduce them to someone you think will be really helpful to achieving their personal objectives in life.

Cash investment: Zero, beyond the cost of a few phone calls.

Strategy 83 – Life is tremendous

"Life Is Tremendous" is the title of a book by a guy called Charlie "Tremendous" Jones. I must admit I've never read his book, but I've always been struck by a fairly well-known quote from it: "You'll be the same person you are today in five years' time, except for the people you meet and the books you read."

That's more profound than it might appear at first.

You see, most of us are set on our path through life and momentum just keeps us going in the direction we've been headed in up till that point. That's basis physics — unless something makes us re-think what we've been doing and where we're trying to get to, we'll keep going the way we always have.

Hollywood movies are full of tales of how chance encounters turn people's lives around, as are novels, plays, songs, poems and just about every other sort of artistic endeavour you can imagine.

That's no accident. That really is how the world works for 99.999% of us.

Don't let stories of the person who decided what they wanted to do with their live age 12 and pursued that objective doggedly for the next 20 years until they got what they wanted shade your thinking. Very few people succeed at anything that way.

And even fewer do so without meeting a mentor along the way or a wise advisor who helps them realise something which leads to the slight change of tack which ultimately accounts for the bulk of their success.

Sheer luck plays a bigger part in success than people you admire like to admit. They'd rather be heroes on a pedestal all by themselves than share the bragging rights.

However, you can fix the odds of sheer luck striking a little if you think about the people you'd like to meet and the books you might read, as Charlie "Tremendous" Jones might put it.

Books taught me things I never learned in any class I attended. Most people I know haven't read my favourite books, even though I tell them I can trace my success directly to what just five books taught me. I see the world differently in no small part because I was lucky enough to stumble across these books. Here they are…

"The Fifth Discipline" — Peter Senge. A wonderful introduction to the world of systems thinking, which shows you why things don't work as you'd hope they might, and what to do about it.

"Fooled By Randomness" — Nicholas Nassem Taleb. A former options trader's view of how people think about numbers and statistics in completely the wrong way, nearly all the time.

"Customer Satisfaction Is Worthless, Customer Loyalty Is Priceless" — Jeffrey Gitomer. The difference between "meh…OK" and "happy" is the distance between poverty and your fortune. Emotions rule the business world, much as most of us like to pretend they don't.

"Out Of The Crisis" — W Edwards Deming. How to reduce costs and improve quality at the same time by the man whose teachings led to the Japanese car industry going from bombed-out factories in the aftermath of World War 2, to becoming the world's pre-eminent auto manufacturers in a few short decades.

'Predatory Thinking" — Dave Trott. A legendary ad-man shows how thinking differently about problems gives anyone the edge they need to win, no matter how well-resourced and well-respected their competition.

Five books. Perhaps £5-10 each on Amazon for a used copy. Between them, they accounted for most of the success I've known in life.

And you'll notice something important. None of them are about accounting.

I already know more about accounting than 99% of the population — which isn't arrogance, but when you've been a qualified accountant for as long as I have, you'd probably expect me to know a lot more than a member of the public chosen at random.

Often, the additional value I offer my clients isn't in me trying to become a better accountant than 99.9% of the population instead of just 99%.

However, I can add a lot of value by bringing perspectives clients almost certainly haven't considered up to that point in time, wedded to by existing accounting knowledge base and an understanding of their business.

Yes, I became a better person through the people I met too, but that's a longer-term and less certain project. In less than five minutes on Amazon you can find all those books and get them on the way to you. You're in control of that part of your personal growth, and it's just about the most powerful, high-RoI thing you could do for your business.

So why not come and meet me right now inside our Cash Flow Mastery programme? Full details at the end of this book if you want to make your business tremendous.

Time investment: Five minutes to order the books. A few hours to read each of them.

Cash investment: That depends on whether you get new or used copies, but somewhere around £50 should be enough to get you started, especially if you opt for digital editions where they're available.

Strategy 84 – Get your kicks on Route 66

This has nothing to do with the Rolling Stones' song. But it's got everything to do with a Minneapolis-based envelope manufacturer called Harvey Mackay.

Harvey Mackay took over a bankrupt envelope manufacturing business and turned it into a $100 million operation in a few years. He's also written several books and has a gift for selecting attention-grabbing book titles, including the memorably titled "Dig Your Well Before You're Thirsty" and "Beware The Naked Man Who Offers You His Shirt".

All his books are well worth a read, but for our purposes today, one tool Harvey Mackay developed is the focus of our attention. That's called the Mackay 66, the full version of which appears in another of his imaginatively titled books, "Swim With The Sharks Without Being Eaten Alive".

The whole premise of the Mackay 66 is that the better you know your customer, the more likely you are to win the sale and the less likely you are to lose the business to a competitor. So he developed a list of 66 question which, if a salesperson could answer every single one, meant they'd taken the time to understand their customer and form a personal relationship with them.

Some of the questions are fairly obvious — their spouse's name, their kids' names, where they went to university, and so on.

However, there are some are pretty deep in questions in there too. The sort of question you might not immediately think about...and indeed questions whose answers it might be better not to keep in your corporate CRM system.

These include the extent to which your customer is a people-pleaser or someone who makes up their own mind.

Whether they behave ethically, and you can take them at their word.

Whether the customer has the best interests of their business at heart or they're pursuing their own personal self-interest instead.

The key to the Mackay 66 isn't just in the answers to the questions. It's in the fact that in the course of a formal business meeting there is no way the conversation is going to go anywhere near some of the topics in the Mackay 66.

In fact, some wouldn't even be covered in a social conversation outside work and even if you ask the questions outright, you'd be unlikely to get a straight answer.

The secret power of the Mackay 66 isn't the questions. It's the depth of connection you need to form with your customer before they might share a crucial perspective which gives the answer to one of those questions you can't ask outright.

If you watch what your customers say, what they don't say, and how they typically behave in a range of different situations over a period of time you'll know the sort of person they really are, and you'll have all the answers you need for the Mackay 66.

That, in turn, gives you all the information you need to understand how best to sell to them now and how to keep their business in the long-term.

Getting close to your customer costs nothing, apart from a little bit of time, and remembering what they say.

The alternative is behaving like a business contact of mine. I've known him for years, but he insists on calling me "Andrew", although that's not my name, and he sends emails addressed to "Dear Andrew" even though the very act of typing my email address in the "To" box would show him Andrew is not my name at all.

In the early days, I gently corrected him when he greeted me in public with his customary "Hi Andrew!" but he never paid the slightest attention, so I gave up trying to correct him after a while. My emails have my full name prominently displayed. This sort of thing isn't hard.

If you don't think getting close to customers is important, let me flip that around for you.

If you don't get close to your customers...doing things, perhaps, like consistently calling them by a name that's not their own...how likely are they to believe you're the sort of "detail-orientated person who's passionate about customer service" (as my business contact likes to describe himself)?

He's either delusional or, perhaps worse, genuinely thinks he is providing a great service.

He may well do so, but I'll never find out.

I can cope with the personal slight...I've got two commonly mis-spelled names, so I'm never bothered when someone gets one or both of them wrong. In fact, an amazing number of people do call me Andrew when I first meet them, for reasons I can't quite fathom, although most of them quickly call me by my proper name thereafter because they've done things like actually read my business card or noticed, when responding to an email, that Andrew isn't my name.

It seems pretty clear to me that anyone who's been told as many times as this business contact of mine that my name isn't Andrew, yet still calls me that, spends no time at all thinking about me or my business.

Getting close to your customers matters. The Mackay 66 is a great way to do it. And it costs nothing to lock in long-term customer relationships when you do it right.

Time investment: A few minutes here and there over time, as part of a conversation you're having anyway. You won't get all the Mackay answers quickly and you shouldn't try to. Some questions can be asked directly, others you'll just need to put in the time to watch and listen. But they'll build up an unrivalled picture of your customer which you can use to build your business by serving them better.

Cash investment: Nothing — it doesn't cost any extra to find out the answers to some of these questions in the course of a meeting you're having anyway.

Strategy 85 – Goals: A help or a hindrance?

The basic template for advice from management gurus is for businesses to set really specific challenging goals and then run their people hard to deliver them.

Whilst this concept has something to commend it, the practical implications aren't always as neat and pretty as you might imagine.

Give someone a specific challenging goal and organise your incentive schemes around delivering, or preferably exceeding, those outcomes and you're right about one thing – most people will do everything they can think of to deliver the outcomes you demanded.

There's just one problem with that – a problem that's magnified if their ability to keep their job depends on delivering those outcomes. And that's the fact that most people will do everything they can think of to deliver the outcomes you demanded.

People will cut corners...cheat even...to make sure they keep their jobs and secure their bonus. No short-term decision is too short-term in that environment. Can customers be manipulated, lied to or pressurised just to make a sale?

Too right they can. And at least a significant number of your people will do exactly that if you pile enough pressure on. In some organisations that toxic culture seeps right through the organisation and poisons everyone involved with is.

Recently Wells Fargo, one of the oldest banks in the US, had its reputation trashed when it turned out that in a "ruthless, target-driven culture" bank employees opened fake accounts to hit their targets, mis-sold products to customers and made transfers to different accounts without their customers' consent.

At the time of writing, this has led to fines and penalties of somewhere around $3 billion. The top management has been cleared out and, in some cases, past bonuses clawed back from senior executives. Thousands of rank-and-file employees have lost their jobs and their stock price collapsed.

All because of the way goals were set and managed.

So what can you do instead? Arizona State University researchers discovered that people who are set outcome-based goals tend to operate in what they called a "prevention focus", that is they operated in such a way as to avoid negative outcomes (such as being fired for underperformance). In tests, 61% of people given an outcome goal inflated their results to avoid falling short.

The rate was one-third lower in people given a learning goal instead of an outcome goal. Instead of a sales target of £X, you might give your staff a learning objective instead. Completing the Mackay 66 might be something to consider because getting close enough to customers to answer all 66 questions means more sales are likely to follow in the fullness of time.

You see, as the business owner you own the outcomes, not your staff. It might be satisfying to fire someone who wasn't making their sales targets, but what if the real problem was that your products of your offer wasn't attractive enough to the customers?

What if the real problem is that the marketing materials weren't strong enough, or the pricing wasn't right, or the target identification missed the mark?

Even good people under pressure to pay their mortgage, like the staff at Wells Fargo, will push things too far if their jobs depend on hitting a particular target.

But long after you've fired them, you'll be left handling the problems caused by customers who feel mis-sold to, who don't feel your business has supported them the way you promised and who feel ripped off in some way.

The impact of those costs lingers for a lot longer than the time it takes to fire someone...and costs a good deal more into the bargain.

Relentless pressure to meet short-term targets is a counterproductive tactic for any business and always leads to higher costs in the long run.

While the $3 billion Wells Fargo shelled out is an extreme example, there are costs everywhere for pursuing arbitrary goals too rigorously. It's just that you won't know what most of them are until long after the people responsible have left your business and you're cleaning up the mess they left behind.

If you're not getting the results you hoped for, that doesn't necessarily mean the people concerned have done anything wrong. Nearly always, they've done the best they can with the skills and expertise at their disposal.

It might be time to reconsider either the goal itself or at least the process by which you hope to get there.

And before you get the P45s out if your goal isn't getting delivered right on schedule, just remember that ramping up the pressure on your people is unlikely to get you any closer — or if it does you might be storing up all sorts of hidden costs down the line you can't see at the moment.

You save significant amounts of cash by not persevering with something that isn't working. As Einstein said, the definition of insanity is doing the same thing over and over again and expecting different results.

Once you're tried your best, it's time for a re-think. Your business will thank you, and so will your cash flow...both immediately in not throwing good money after bad, and in the long term by not having to compensate customers who have been mis-sold.

Knowing the right targets to set and setting them in the right way is one of the key components of the Cash Flow Mastery programme. With the right business model in place and the right targets to back it up, managing your business cash flow becomes an order of magnitude easier because everyone is pulling in the direction most likely to make you more money.

Time investment: Nothing — not continuing to do something that clearly isn't working saves you time.

Cash investment: Zero. You're not wasting your cash in the short term, and you're maximising repeat purchases and revenues in the long run by not treating customers like disposable commodities. So you're ahead of the game right out the starting blocks.

Strategy 86 – Segmenting your customers the right way

There's some dispute between people who care about this sort of thing as to whether it was Mark Twain or UK Prime Minister Benjamin Disraeli who first said, "There are three kinds of lies: lies, damned lies and statistics."

For our purposes, though, it doesn't really matter who said it, just that it's a useful rule to keep in mind.

And, to be fair, more often than not, it's less about people lying to you and more to do with the fact that very few people understand how statistics work. Most often, they grab at a figure which seems to prove the point they wanted to make and declare, "statistics show that…".

It doesn't necessarily get any better by being more sophisticated. Often, that confuses the issue even further.

Let's consider a common technique — segmenting your customer base into different groups with similar characteristics.

Marketing departments do this sort of thing all the time. And there's a comforting "obviousness" about it — wouldn't you want to market differently to men, as opposed to women, for example? Or young people differently from old people? Or wealthy people differently to poor people?

That's the promise of many popular advertising platforms nowadays — the micro-targeting of your customer base.

Let's say you've got 1000 female customers and your marketing manager tells you of some great new wheeze they've come across. They've tried this out with 12 customers selected at random and they all bought what you were selling. Now your marketing manager wants to flip the switch and serve that same ad to all 1000 of your female customers.

Should you say yes?

The 100% record is interesting as far as it goes, but this represents a sample of just 1.2% of the available audience. So your first instinct should be to question how valid the experience of that sample was (and for extra points, exactly how the "random" selection was done – only rarely is something described as a random example anything of the sort).

Statistics only really works with large numbers of people. You need hundreds or thousands of answers to accurately gauge the response rate on an ongoing basis.

And that's because people are all different, notwithstanding where we went to school, how much we earn or what gender we represent.

In fact, for many products there are more similarities between groups than you might expect. 40- year-old working women have a lot in common with both 40-year-old women who don't work, as well as 40-year-old men who do work, even though those would typically be different groups on your marketing database.

Trouble is, you're looking at the world from your perspective, using characteristics you can easily identify (age, gender, etc), you're not looking at it from your customer's perspective.

They might see themselves as "coffee drinkers" who visit Starbucks every day for breakfast, alongside a lot of other men and women of all ages and backgrounds who do exactly the same. Your category isn't "females aged 18-34", it's "coffee drinkers who are happy to pay £3 for a coffee every morning".

That might lead you to think "affluent consumers" but you'd be wrong – but there's an argument that a daily Starbucks is more in the "affordable treat" category that all sorts of people choose to spend their money on.

Once you've made the leap to thinking about your customers differently, you'll see the world in a different light.

Maybe you invested fortunes in targeted marketing designed to reach women aged 18-34 and sell your coffee. But many people in that age group...those who don't like coffee...will oblivious to your marketing and ignore it. You spent money you didn't need to spend trying to reach people who would never be interested in your product because they don't like coffee.

Or you could have focused your marketing on coffee drinkers, of all ages, genders and levels of affluence. They might be a little harder to find, but the effort is usually worth it as they will be vastly more interested in what you sell. That makes your conversion rates much higher for the same spend, and therefore every sale you make is more profitable.

The key here is to think about your customers the way they think about themselves — coffee drinker, cat person, savoury snack junkie — and stay away from lazy segmentation techniques which have passed their prime.

Once you have an insight into how your customers think about themselves, you have a window into a community of like-minded people who will be more receptive to your offer than customer segmentation based on lazy generalisations will ever be. And because they're more receptive to your offer, you make more sales for every pound you spend on marketing, saving you money and adding to your bottom line.

You save money by not wasting your marketing budget on people who won't convert as readily, if at all, by taking the blinkers off and thinking about your customers the way they think about themselves.

Time investment: Nothing, over and above the time you're already spending on customer segmentation. This is just a different perspective on the same technique.

Cash investment: Zero, for the same reason.

Strategy 87 – Who are you networking with...and why?

Most people hate networking, especially in the sort of organised meetings which are a feature of many business people's breakfasts, lunches and dinners.

Some attendees are over-keen to make a sale and prowl round like a lion circling their prey until they find a weak member of the herd and pounce.

Others have been told they have to be there by their boss, so reluctantly attend, but without any evident enthusiasm or, often, even speaking to anyone unless they already know them.

Networking meetings are also a bit of a "needle in a haystack" when it comes to finding customers you can sell to. Odds are slim that you'll stumble across people who are guaranteed to need your services, unless you offer a service so universal everyone in business is going to need it, such as a bank.

Here's what I do at networking meetings instead of trying, and usually failing, to make a sale because the person I'm talking with is almost by definition unlikely to be an ideal customer for me.

I don't go to networking meetings to find new customers. I go to networking meetings to get connected with people who are probably connected with my ideal customers already.

It so happens that for what I do banks, lawyers, accountants and financial advisors are my most likely source of an introduction or referral. And if I come across one of those, of course they get the 30-second commercial and I usually arrange a follow-up conversation with them.

But if, as is much more likely, I'm talking with someone who doesn't work in those professions, I know they will nearly all have a lawyer, accountant, bank and financial advisor already. So I don't try to sell to the person I'm talking to. What I do instead is ask if they can connect me with their lawyer, accountant or financial advisor.

If I made a sales pitch to every person I met at a networking event, my success rate would be somewhere between zero and not very much. But when I ask someone if they can put me in touch with their accountant or lawyer, the answer is nearly always yes.

Frankly, they're probably delighted that I didn't try to pitch them, like just about everyone else in the room will have done. And most people are happy to help another person out, as long as they're not being asked to do anything too high-risk, in terms of reputation or financial outlay.

In that context, I'm a low risk so most people are happy to make the introduction. I follow up and then have the chance to get one step closer to one of my ideal customers through the other clients of the lawyer, accountant, bank manager or financial advisor I'm talking to.

Once I've explained who I am and what I do they do all the sifting of potential customers on my behalf and they also know that if I come across a client of mine who needs the sort of professional expertise they provide, I'll do the same favour in reverse if I think that's in the client's best interests. So, there's always upside for them too.

At networking events, try not to go in with the mindset that you're there to make a sale...although if by chance you bump into someone who would be an ideal customer by all means pursue the opportunity.

Instead, think about who you can connect with at the networking event who might be able to put you one step closer to your ideal customer. There will be people for you, just like the lawyers and accountants are for me, who will be the perfect intermediary between you and the customer you really want.

Set out to find those people and you'll get much more value out of networking events and, apart from a little bit of time, it won't cost you

Cash Flow Surge

anything to get closer to your potential customers. Done right, you can come away with five or six potential intermediaries in the course of an hour or two which would have taken days to connect with any other way.

This approach to networking gets you closer to your ideal customers faster, and at a lower cost than most other ways of marketing to them which means you keep more of your cash in your own bank account instead of spending it on marketing.

Fast growth at low cost is the holy grail of business development. That's what you can have when you do your networking the right way.

Time investment: A couple of hours at a networking meeting every now and again.

Cash investment: Often completely free, but occasionally a nominal outlay to cover the cost of your breakfast, lunch, etc. When you network right, that modest investment always pays itself back many times over.

Strategy 88 – Beware the budget

You might think this is a slightly unusual thing for an accountant to say, but budgets don't help your business as much as you might think they do...or as much as most accountants tell you they will.

There's nothing wrong with thinking ahead and planning for the future. Far from it. But doing a budget once a year which is then used to control every aspect of your business for the following 12 months can often cause more problems than it solves.

That's because the world changes a lot faster than once a year for most businesses I come across. Nowadays, the business world seems to turn upside down several times a year rather than every few years, like it used to.

As a result, most business's planning cycles are now well out of kilter with their operating cycles, which can be fatal in today's fast-paced world.

Think about it. If the world your business operates in changes on a weekly basis, but you only change your budgets once a year, that means for 51 weeks out of every year you're operating on out of date information. And that's even worse than it sounds because the compounding effect as each fresh week goes by means another change beds into your marketplace and you're even more out of date than you were last week.

To run a successful business, your planning timescale and your operating timescale need to be aligned as closely as possible to make sure you don't get so far out of kilter with the rest of the world you operate within that there's no way back to where you need to be to remain competitive.

Now, banks and auditors still rather like to see annual budgets, so you might as well do one. It also helps you get the right operational structure in place, identify your fixed and variable costs and sort out your target margins, so this exercise isn't completely wasted.

For now, though, I'm going to share with you an approach I use with clients. You'll hear more about this if you choose to come on the Cash Flow Mastery programme, but this is the way I help business owners keep their business and cash flow on track.

I call it the 6-3-1 fine-tuning system.

That is, at the halfway point of their financial year (month 6), I essentially re-do the annual plan again and alter the forecast year-end outturn accordingly. I call this the mid-year reforecast and report results for the second half of the year against both the original budget and the reforecast so the business can see what's changed.

Every quarter (month 3) I check the major variables, depending on the client's business model. There's usually a couple of factors that matter more than any other — the cost of customer acquisition, perhaps, or the machine utilisation rates in a manufacturing operation, for example.

If they're not pretty much on track, I do a bit of a deep dive on those to work out what's going on and adjust the forecast for remainder of the year if the changes look like they're here to stay.

Finally, every month, I adjust the expectations for the year ahead bearing in mind what we've learned in the last month.

That might be a simple as a major project being deferred from one month to the next, or it could be something like the loss of a major customer which would have a material impact on the client's results for the year.

While that sounds like a lot of extra work, once you've got the annual budget framework in place to give a structure to your plans for the year, this is less work than it might sound at first.

As you're focusing on some quite specific things at the 6-3-1 milestones, the whole process only takes a couple of hours a month.

There is also the considerable advantage that are you aren't letting people spend against annual budgets without considering changes in the business environment you operate in. Nor are people hampered by their original budgets if it's necessary to make an urgent change, they just get incorporated into the 6-3-1 reviews at the appropriate time, which is usually soon enough for most purposes.

If you lost a major customer, for example, at no more than a month's notice, you can ramp up your sales and marketing efforts to replace that customer with someone else and consider which parts of your business might need to take a back seat for a little while instead.

Without customers you don't have a business, but could you delay the upgrade to the factory toilets by a couple of months if that made the difference between bringing in enough revenue to keep everyone employed or not? Almost certainly yes. And, handled in the right way, the people in the factory wouldn't even complain about it.

With an annual budget people are either not spending when they should be spending or continuing to spend when they shouldn't. While they serve a purpose, for most businesses annual budgeting cycles are too long in today's more competitive, faster-changing world.

Try the 6-3-1 method instead to keep your planning cycle and your operating cycle in sync. That makes sure your business never gets so far out of kilter it can't be brought back in line again before it's too late.

Time investment: A couple of hours a month.

Cash investment: Zero — and if it means you stop spending on things that have stopped working and start spending on new priorities faster than you would have done otherwise, that's a net benefit to both your bottom line and your bank balance at the same time.

Strategy 89 – When to cut your losses...and when to double-down

You already know that cutting losses is the smart thing to do, irrespective of how much time and effort you've already put into a project. There are a couple of subtleties to this, though.

Firstly, you need to distinguish between situations that ***could*** be resolved positively, even though they're not looking good right now, and those which stand no chance of a successful resolution.

I recently worked with a client to help them understand that, in a particular market they served, there was no way they could ever hope to make a profit — their cost base was far too high relative to the price the market was prepared to pay. Their cost base couldn't be reduced significantly and there was no other way to build in differentiation in a relatively low-priced commodity product at a higher price which customers were prepared to pay.

The smart decision here was just to accept the situation and shut the operation down.

But, for another client who has a loss-making division, I was able to show them that each job they did was individually profitable. Their problem was that they just didn't have enough jobs coming through each week to cover their overheads with the profits they made on the jobs which had passed through the factory.

Unlike the first client, they could make the operation profitable. The fundamental economics of their proposition were sound, they just needed to improve the effectiveness of their sales and marketing, and they'd be fine.

But if that's when you should cut your losses, when should you double-down on your plans?

One of my favourite examples is from Jesse Livermore, who was something of an icon in the investment world during the early part of the 20th century.

He traded his way from penniless street-urchin to billionaire (in today's money) in stocks and commodities between the early 1900s and the 1940s, riding his way up and down the financial crashes and depressions along the way.

One of his techniques was to invest in a stock and if the stock moved in the right direction, he'd immediately add to his investment as that showed him his instinct was right. Conversely, if the stock moved against the trade, he'd immediately close his position to preserve his capital.

Jesse Livermore became a modern-day billionaire by letting his winning positions run until they stopped making incremental profits.

And that's something many businesses forget.

They need more sales, so they invest, say, £1000 a month in advertising. Most businesses are happy if that investment returns a positive RoI, so they give the marketing department a £1000 per month budget and keep it rolling over from one month to the next.

Here's what they should do instead. If they invest £1000 per month in advertising and it brings in a multiple of that investment in relatively short order, they should increase the budget to £1500. Then to £2000, and so on until the investment stops bringing in more than it costs to run.

I've almost never seen a business do this. If they make a return on their £1000, their Finance Director or CFO is happy, and the marketing manager gets to boast of a positive outcome. They're both happy...but they're both leaving money on the table.

If you want to grow your business, and a £1000 investment brings in more income than it costs to run, why wouldn't you spend 10 grand to generate 20 grand...a million quid to generate two million...a billion quid to generate two billion, if you could.

It's not a traditional budget setting approach, but that's how Jesse Livermore became a billionaire.

All he was doing was betting on outcomes he knew were more or less "dead certs" because he'd already been proved right in his judgement — if he thought the stock price would go up, and it did, so it was likely to keep moving in that direction until the point where he could bank big profits.

Next time you see something working like this, why not double up on your successes just as rigorously as you cut your losses. Wherever you're headed, you'll get there a lot faster and with a lot less risk into the bargain.

Time investment: None, beyond the time you'd have spent anyway reviewing business performance.

Cash investment: None, once you know you're doing something with a pretty much guaranteed RoI. Yes, you have to cash flow the initial investment, but if it pays back quickly and reliably, that minor short-term cash flow impact will quickly repay itself.

Strategy 90 – We hit our delivery KPIs, but all the customers are furious…how did that happen?

The target for delivery was 15 days.

The delivery KPI reported in the monthly board pack was 15 days.

And yet increasingly irascible customer complaints about deliveries were piling up on the CEO's desk. How could that happen when the business was hitting its KPIs?

This was the mystery facing Jack Welch early in his career as CEO at GE, with one of their most important divisions. Jack Welch hadn't yet earned the reputation as one of the 20th century's most successful business leaders, but he wanted to know more….so he started digging.

It's worth bearing in mind that GE sold industrial equipment. Big hunks of metal that took time to manufacture and dispatch. Waiting 15 days for delivery wasn't a big deal to their customers and they were happy to do so as they often had other parts of their own internal supply chain which were set up to align with deliveries from GE. The 15-day lead time gave them an opportunity to organise the project within their own business.

As it turns out, the problem was that, although GE's average delivery time was indeed 15 days, that masked huge swings in actual delivery times.

Some customers got their delivery in a couple of days and then had to store bulky manufactured components for another couple of weeks until the rest of the bits needed for their project turned up, which was very inconvenient.

Meanwhile, other customers waited nearly a month for their deliveries, long past the indicated 15 days at the time of quotation. So, they had to store the parts all the other suppliers delivered until GE's piece of the jigsaw turned up and they could get on with the job in hand.

Almost no customers got their delivery in 15 days, and just because a customer got a 2-day delivery last time, there was no guarantee they'd get the same next time. Theirs could easily be one of the 4-week deliveries next time around.

It was no wonder pretty much all the customers were unhappy. This was little better than chaos, even though all the internal KPIs at GE were met.

There, of course, also a story in here about how you set internal KPIs, which most organisations do really badly, but that's not what we're talking about here. For now, all I'll say is that the right KPIs are a key element of getting your business model generating cash for you, rather than draining cash out your business. That's why we cover this in-depth in our Cash Flow Mastery programme — full details at the end of this book.

Going back to Jack Welch, though, his solution was not to change the average KPI, which remained at 15 days, but it was to get the deliveries turning up **on** Day 15, not round and about, certainly not 4 weeks, but not 2 days either. 15 days exactly.

Within a short period of time the customers were happy again. They got what they paid for — the 15-day delivery service. And that service was reliable in that it was virtually always 15 days, with a high degree of certainty. Customers could plan their project delivery around the firm expectation that GE's delivery would turn up like clockwork on Day 15.

This matters because most internal KPIs are set as averages, as GE's was before Jack Welch got involved. However, customers don't care about averages, they only care about their own experience.

If you commute by train, you don't care all that much about the train company's claim of an average 91.7% on-time arrival if your own experience is that the train you catch every morning is always 20 minutes late.

If your bank claims to answer the phone in three rings, on average, but you always seem to be on hold for 10 minutes or more, it's your experience which determines your level of satisfaction with your bank, not what the average experience is out of the thousands of customers who call that bank every month.

If anything, knowing that, on average, very few people get as bad a service as you get is only likely to irritate you even more...most people would wonder why, if 9 out of 10 trains get where they're supposed to on time, why are they "picking on you" by making sure your train one of the few that always comes in late? It's not likely to garner positive reviews or ensure customer loyalty, that's for sure.

This works through to your cash flow.

Most people would be prepared to pay more for a reliable service, one that never lets them down, one they can bank on.

When deliveries are often late or unpredictable, most people would build in a bit of headroom on the price in case they need to store a delivery somewhere or hold up production until your part turns up.

If you want to get top dollar, you need to ensure you're an utterly reliable supplier of whatever your business provides.

And the secret to that is to ignore the averages and work to reduce the distribution between the highs and lows of your service.

To use the GE example, once every delivery is one exactly 15 days you can spend some time and effort reducing the average to a smaller number than that and sell the benefits of faster turnarounds to your customers in a positive — and perhaps price-enhancing — way. Until then average matters a lot less than how big the disparity between best and worst is.

Time investment: A few minutes here and there. Every time you're told that such-and-such a thing happens in an average of X days, just ask what the longest and the shortest amount of time it might take. Don't fall for

241

bland assurances that everything is fine — get the exact numbers. The bigger the difference between highest and lowest, the more likely it is that something's going badly wrong...and I can guarantee your customers will have noticed, so get fixing it as soon as you can to protect your cash flow.

Cash investment: Zero. It costs nothing beyond the salaries you're already paying to get this information.

Strategy 91 – Reading between the lines

I did a law degree at university before being seduced by the bright lights of a career in accounting. Having a law degree has often been quite helpful, and not only because now I know what lawyers are talking about when they update me on a case they're handling.

It's helpful because of the way it taught me to think. One of the classes I got the most out of was the Law of Evidence, which is all about how you prove your case in a courtroom.

Ideally you want plenty of direct evidence that something has happened — fingerprints at the scene, DNA evidence, that sort of thing. Perhaps a couple of highly credible witnesses who are prepared to swear under oath that they saw the accused speeding away from the crime scene in a stolen car. The presence of a motive.

We were all taught that there's a hierarchy of evidence which runs from the accused ending someone's life by their own hand in front of a roomful of independent witnesses, with ample corroborating physical evidence and the presence of a motive, all the way down to a couple of people speculating in a pub a few weeks later on the reasons why the accused might have "done their victim in".

Once you know what a real body of evidence looks like, it's very easy to become unimpressed with most business cases for spending money on something.

A few anecdotes, a quote from Forbes or Inc Magazine...or worse, a statement from a clearly self-interested professional body...and a quick spreadsheet with some costings doesn't come close to the sort of evidence 'd be looking for to sanction a business case.

 might not mind quite so much if the opening line at the pitch was "...this is highly speculative, but we think it's worth a try..." At least that's honest.

But if you think a wish list and a few bits of information which mildly point in the direction you've already decided to take is going to convince me in a hurry, you're sadly mistaken.

In business, we all need to take a punt from time to time. As long as everyone knows that's what we're doing, I'm more than happy.

I'm not against innovation. Just against people pretending wild bets are racing certainties when they're clearly anything but.

So next time you're presented with a business case to spend money, read between the lines a little.

If the business case is the equivalent of two people down the pub speculating as to who might have committed the crime, don't spend a penny making that happen.

If there's solid evidence of, firstly, a genuine customer need for whatever is being proposed, and secondly that the proposed solution is the best way of addressing that need, then fill your boots.

Solid evidence doesn't mean a survey in a third-tier business publication stating that 83% of millennials prefer to communicate via social media, or some such nonsense. That's more or less equivalent to two people talking down the pub, speculating who might have "done him in".

Nor does it mean that citing a report by , say, the CIPD (the HR managers' trade body) which says every business will need an HR Director on the future or that your business will fail if you don't employ a Diversity Officer right away.

That's not to say your business doesn't need either of those things, it's just that they're clearly invested in a particular outcome as that would benefit their members most. They are not independent witnesses, no matter how much they dress up their claims with credible sounding policy statements and a range of data points.

Nor does solid evidence mean the number of social media mentions of blockchain or bitcoin. All that means is that lots of people while away their time speculating about those subjects. It doesn't necessarily mean you should spend any time or money on those initiatives yourself.

Next time you're asked to put your hand in your pocket for some of your hard-earned cash to kick-start a project, imagine the proposal was a legal case.

Would you vote to convict someone on the strength of the evidence presented? Think like a lawyer for the other side — how would you unpick this for a jury? Where is the evidence weak? Have they presented enough independent sources of evidence that the case is overwhelming, or is it just idle speculation which, in all probability, means nothing?

Get that call right and you keep a lot more cash in your own bank account and make sure other people don't fritter your company funds on projects designed to enhance their careers without impacting your bottom line.

Time investment: A few minutes every time you're presented with an investment proposal. But it won't take much longer than you'd spend reading the proposal anyway — you'll quickly find the bits that are missing if you think like a lawyer and can send your people on their way to make a better case without taking up too much of your time.

Cash investment: Zero. This keeps money in your bank account, rather than spending it when the changes of success are low.

Strategy 92 – The 80% technique

Handelsbanken is a well-known name in UK financial circles now, but it could easily have been a name we'd never heard of.

Following a major financial crisis in the early 1970s the bank, then known as Svenska Handelsbanken, needed radical surgery to restore its fortunes. The board appointed the then fairly young Jan Wallander to the top job in order to sort things out.

He took a very radical path which lives on till this day, including an emphasis on the importance of physical branches at a time other banks were (and still are) retrenching their operations and the "church spire" concept, which means every branch should only serve customers within the distance it can see from the top of the town's church spire. They make a great virtue out of being hyper-local at a time other banks are become more anonymous and centralised.

Jan Wallander did a number of very clever things, but the one we're talking about here was the way he restructured the bank's operations.

As is quite normal in a restructuring process, there is a big focus on the people in the business, how much time they need to do their jobs and how many of them the business might be able to do without.

The usual approach is to max out everyone's time and make sure people are hyper-busy to reduce operating costs and, to use a horrible expression, "sweat the assets".

Jan Wallander was much smarter than the average restructuring CEO, though.

Although he led the bank through pretty much the same exercise, he only filled up 80% of his staff's time. That was because he knew things would come along which hadn't been expected, that sometimes two customers would want something doing on the same day at the same time or that a job would take longer than anticipated for any one of a number of reasons.

For sure, he had an eye on the bank's operating costs today. But he had a bigger focus on the operating costs in the future...after the restructuring was completed and the bank knew it would live to fight another day.

Jan Wallander prioritised serving quickly and efficiently and knew that meant his staff needed to have the time to do their very best for each customer or he wouldn't have a bank to run for very long. Handelsbanken would just become another anonymous big bank with very few positive features to the experience of being a customer there.

Less insightful CEOs would have filled up the extra 20% of their staff's time, but Jan Wallander knew it would be harder to acquire future new customers in the face of poor reviews and people moaning to their family and friends about the poor service they'd received.

It would mean more mistakes in the short-term, leading to more credits and compensation payments.

It would lead to a more pressurised, less engaged group of staff who would just be "going through the motions" rather than demonstrating they had the best interests of their customers at heart by their actions.

If any of those things had happened, Handelsbanken would have suffered a much higher rate of customer churn, which in turn means Jan Wallander would have needed to invest more of the money he didn't have to bring in new customers at a faster rate than customers left the bank. That's always an expensive way to run a business.

As it happens, Jan Wallander led Handelsbanken to a period of unprecedented prosperity. Over the past few years Handelsbanken has led the customer service league tables amongst banks and been consistently above the average of the banking sector for its profits.

And all this was achieved by ***not*** loading up every minute of every day for every member of staff. Rather Handelsbanken has achieved its impressive results by giving their staff the time to do a first-rate professional job. Over the last four decades it's allowed Handelsbanken to become one of the most profitable banks on the planet.

You can do the same quite easily, just by thinking differently about how your people can add more value to your customers to earn their long-term loyalty, and just as importantly, securing your long-term cash flow.

Time investment: In reality, none. You'll be collecting and analysing the same data either way.

Cash investment: in the very short term, traditional accounting metrics will show you running at a slightly higher level of cost than the "scorched earth" approach might suggest. But you'll do that at the expense of losing customers and thereby having to increase your marketing and business development costs to keep the flow of new business coming to fill up the gaps in your future income stream. This approach means you're ultimately saving money, not spending it.

Strategy 93 – The mathematics of good customer service

While some business owners regard good customer service as an unnecessary luxury, smart business owners recognise any costs are far outweighed by increased profits.

But I recognise some people are sceptical, so let's do the maths.

Clearly you'll need to plug in your own numbers, but let's take some pretty common margins and imagine a business with its cost of sales at 50% of income (i.e. it makes a gross margin of 50%) and that salaries and overheads consume 40% of sales, leaving a profit of 10%. Most businesses would be quite happy to make a steady 10% on the bottom line.

To put that into monetary terms, if the business had a client who paid them £10,000 per year, on average, they'd bring in £5,000 in gross profit for the business and deliver £1,000 of net profit after paying out their share of the overheads, i.e. £4,000.

If your business keeps this client for a year, how much are they worth? £1,000 obviously, in this somewhat over-simplified example. That's the margin after accounting for all the costs of providing your products and services to them.

Should this client use your services for a year and then go elsewhere, they're worth £1,000 to you.

But if you kept them for an extra year what are they worth? Well £2,000 on that basis (there is an argument that this client is worth more than that, but we're keeping the example simple for now – just accept it's worth at least £2,000 and could well be worth more, for the purposes of this example).

So even if you invested a fairly miserly 2% of your sales income in providing great customer service over that two-year period, you're still £600 ahead —

i.e. the £1,000 in extra net profit from the additional, less the £400 (2% of 2 x £10,000=£400) over two years that it cost to keep the customer on-board.

You make back one-and-a-half times your customer service investment in just two years, which is a rate of return you'll struggle to find from most other investments you could make.

Better than that, as returns on investment go, this is a fairly "dead cert" investment. You're much more likely to see a positive return because all the factors of how you go about serving your customers are under your control.

You certainly have a good deal more control over how you service an existing customer versus trying to sign up a new customer you've never dealt with before who might, or might not, bring in the same level of profits.

And if it works in Year 2, it will probably work in Year 3, Year 4 and so on into the future. Of course, some customers will drift away for all sorts of reasons whatever you do, but it's not hard to get a positive financial return out of good customer service even factoring in customer losses as the numbers are so heavily skewed in your favour.

Great service also increases the likelihood that your customers will make referrals and recommendations for your business to their friends, family and business contacts.

I've done this myself and doubled the size of businesses in a few years just by focusing on customer service. Only rarely did this cost any extra money, more usually it was nothing at all, never mind the £200pa in the example above, which meant that the additional sales income was extremely profitable.

There is just one little trick to this, though. You have to make sure your frontline staff are completely focused on serving the customers. Your systems need to be good, otherwise frontline staff will spend all their time firefighting.

And you need to ruthlessly eliminate all unnecessary distractions — pointless meetings, management systems which eliminate discretion for frontline staff and make sure managers' intervention is for positive reasons, not just demanding yet another status update or holding an hour-long briefing on some new corporate policy when there are customers who need service.

Do that and you can bank a lot of extra cash because you'll be keeping your customers for longer, and for each extra year you keep them, at little or no cost, you get a stream of extra profits in return for investing pennies.

Good customer service has such a positive RoI, I'm always astounded so few businesses seem all that concerned about providing the best service possible.

Businesses providing great customer service stand out in their industry because so few of their competitors even try. That makes it easy to keep a regular and sustainable cash flow going several years longer than a ho-hum service would have done.

A model which brings in substantial extra profits at a cost of little or nothing is the very definition of what we're trying to do round here. Great customer service is one of the best ways there is to get substantial amounts of extra cash into your bank account for an outlay of just pennies. Try it and enjoy the extra cash flow you'll get in return.

Time investment: Little or nothing — his is about how time you're already paying for is being used, not usually about spending more time or increasing costs.

Cash investment: Zero. You're already paying all the salaries in your business. This is just how you prioritise your frontline staff's time.

Strategy 94 – Kintsugi

I'd seen these pieces of art before, but only recently found out what the style was called.

Kintsugi is a Japanese art form made from delicate porcelain bowls which have broken and are re-formed out of the original pieces, the different sections held together with melted gold.

Kintsugi roughly translates as "golden joinery" or "golden repair" and it builds on an element of Japanese philosophy which is all about learning to embrace the imperfect.

In the hands of a skilled craftsperson, kintsugi can transform some broken pottery into an object which is admired even more after it was broken than it was before. If you search online, you'll see some lovely objects made using this technique.

You see, the Japanese have a different philosophy of life. In the West, we'd just throw away a broken cup. They put a considerable amount of effort into fixing it.

In the West, we'd try to make an invisible repair. In Japan they celebrate the imperfections, even highlighting them with molten gold to make the breaks more obvious than they would otherwise be. For a Japanese person, they're celebrating the life of this piece of porcelain, including its cracks and flaws, and accepting it for what it is, with its own story and its own history.

But why does this matter to your cash flow?

Well, often in business we spend a lot of time and effort trying to make something into our image of what perfection should be. We want reliably replicable results for everything we do, and we try to make all experiences in the business uniform and identical, squeezing out all traces of individuality.

Just about every sort of management training programme tries to do this, usually at great expense and generally with questionable results.

Although you'll never hear this from a management training company, most people are very unlikely to move all that much from wherever they are now...certainly not by the time they've got to a level in your organisation where you're investing in management training for them. By then people have generally made their minds up on rather too many things already.

There will be plenty of lip service paid to the process and people will generally be flattered that you're investing a considerable amount of money in their personal development. But that doesn't mean they're going to change deep down inside.

Some do, of course. Some change their behaviour faster than a TV evangelist caught in a compromising position with a parishioner, but most don't.

Instead, how about cutting out a lot of that expensive training and executive coaching and accepting people for who they are, with all their upsides and downsides?

Accept that we're all like those kintsugi bowls. We've all been broken a little in different ways over the years and put ourselves back together again as best we can.

An old colleague of mine paid me a great compliment once. He said I'd assembled the finest group of misfits he'd ever worked with — all the weaknesses cancelled one other out across the whole team but the areas where each brought a phenomenal degree of strength and aptitude were allowed to run to their maximum capability, while their colleagues filled in for one another's blind spots.

We didn't invest in management training in a vain attempt to make people into someone different. We accepted them for who they were and the strengths they brought, then sculpted the business around them.

This business was really effective too. Sales grew threefold in three years and profits soared.

So, think very carefully before you spend money trying to make people into something they're not. Perhaps try accepting them for who they are instead.

Odds are, you'll both be happier.

Time investment: Little or nothing.

Cash investment: Zero. By not wasting money on programmes which promise (but rarely do) transform people you keep more cash within your business. For extra bonus points, invest a little bit of what you save in helping your people become more of who they really are, and you'll still come out ahead.

Strategy 95 – Old and unimproved

Like all Scots, I have a special place in my heart for Irn Bru…like the ads say, Scotland's other national drink.

This supposedly fruit-flavoured drink — although I think most of us would struggle to say precisely what fruit it actually tastes of — has an iconic status in Scotland. So much so, it's one of the few places in the world where Coca Cola isn't the best-selling soft drink.

If you're not a Scot, you'll wonder what all the fuss is about, but somehow Barr's, the makers of Irn Bru have done such a great job of planting their product so firmly in the minds of Scots that we can't get enough of it. There were howls of protest in Scotland when the new sugar tax meant Barr's had to tinker with their long-standing recipe and scale back the industrial quantities of sugar which used to go into every bottle.

The weather in Scotland isn't usually that great so we tend not to be one of the world's more natural "take to the streets" nations. Staying indoors with the fire on tends to be our way of doing things. But changing the Irn Bru recipe elicited the strength of feeling in Scotland which threatened to bring the whole nation out on the streets.

As I was writing this book, Irn Bru came out with another in their long line of marketing masterstrokes and launched a limited edition of their original 1901 recipe for Irn Bru, replete with tons of sugar, just like in the old days.

This sparked what can only be described as a buying frenzy north of the border…not to mention acres of free publicity for Irn Bru itself, multiplying Barr's original marketing investment many times over.

Irn Bru's tag line for the campaign — "Old and Unimproved" is a masterpiece.

Like a lot of their advertising, it's gently humorous and pokes fun at itself as much as anything else. In this instance it also pokes fun at the "new and improved" slogan food and drink manufacturers throw around the supermarket shelves a lot more often than they probably ought to.

There are two lessons from this which directly benefit your cash flow.

Firstly, having an idea as great as "old and unimproved" didn't make their marketing more expensive. It cost no more to print the ads. It took no longer to say in a radio commercial or TV advertisement. But its cheeky approach meant "old and unimproved" Irn Bru multiplied their marketing investment many times over...for free...by making it something the media wrote about.

There's no better way to save money on your marketing budget than by coming up with ideas that keep you in the news. When done well, the press writes about you instead of you having to buy media space to run your ads.

That's hard to do consistently, although Irn Bru is excellent at this. Recently they've been riffing off Kanye West's "Jesus Is King" album release by promoting their own spoof "Ginger Is King" album instead. (Get a friendly Glaswegian to explain the delightful play on words here – space doesn't permit me to do so.)

The second lesson is that sometimes "old and unimproved" would actually be a positive selling point to customers. It sounds counter-intuitive, but things like providing old-fashioned personal service instead of robot scripts in a call centre or sending a handwritten letter instead of an automated email really stands out. Making a virtue of this means your customers identify your business based on not just what you do but how you do it.

Building the sort of raving fans that Irn Bru has garnered over their many years of top-notch marketing is a tall order for anyone to replicate. But just making it clear what you stand for and how you'll treat customers will, in itself, lead to people who want precisely that service beating a path to your door instead of buying from your competitors.

It also makes it much easier to convert a prospect into a new customer, because if you're selling not just what they want, but doing it in a way they find most closely identifies with how they like to be treated...especially when most people don't to it that way...then you're on to a winner.

Don't copy what Irn Bru do. But have a look at the way they've developed their message over the years and how successful that has been. Then develop your own way of taking that principle and test it out with your own customers.

As the world is becoming more bland and businesses in the same sector are harder than ever to tell apart, paradoxically it's easier than it's ever been to stand out from the crowd by doing things differently. In most industries, the bar is set low enough that just about anyone can do it if they put their mind to it.

What's your version of "old and unimproved"? Find that and you're on to a winner.

Time investment: It takes no longer to come up with a stand-out idea than a "same ol' same ol'" one. This is more about having the courage and insight to be different from the rest of your industry, than the time it takes.

Cash investment: it doesn't cost any more to produce ads, point of sale material and anything else you might need with a good tag line on it vs an insipid one. Once you've got your inspiration, this bit's free.

Strategy 96 – How to improve productivity 20-37% without spending a penny

Productivity improvements are always worth pursuing. That's because you're already paying for the people to be at work, so if you get more out each of the working days you're already paying for, and do so without increasing your costs, your cash flow quickly takes a positive turn.

There are two sorts of productivity improvement.

The first is when some consultant comes in and charges you a fortune to tell you that your computer system needs a complete upgrade or all the machines in your factory need replacing.

It's important you've got a weather eye out for those opportunities. Sometimes a radical change or two can dramatically improve the economics of your business. But however successful that change is, it's worth remembering that anyone who sold that package to you is probably going to sell it to all your competitors too. At best you've got a head start, but you won't have an advantage for long.

And, of course, you've got a significant investment programme to fund as well, which makes quite a dent in your cash flow up front, even if you get a return on that investment down the line.

The other sort of productivity improvement costs pretty much nothing up front and none of your competitors can buy the same thing and use it to compete against you. It probably won't surprise you to know that's the sort of productivity improvement we're more keen on around here.

What's more, it's simple to do and takes no more of your time that it takes to run your business now, although you might need to do things differently.

The secret to improving productivity 20-37% is to bring more happiness to your workplace. A study by the Social Market Foundation discovered happier employees were 20% more productive than unhappy ones.

And if you make your sales force happier, according to an article in Forbes magazine, your sales team can be up to 37% more productive than their unhappy colleagues working for your competitors.

I've seen businesses spend millions of pounds spent on new IT systems or upgrading factory equipment justified on the promise of just a 10% improvement in productivity, so 20% or 37% is an astounding result. And you can usually achieve that result spending little or nothing, rather than needing to make multi-million-pound investments.

The RoI on happiness is considerable.

According to Forbes, companies which featured in their 100 Best Companies to Work for List saw stock prices increase by 14% over a seven-year period compared to only 8% for companies which didn't make the list – that's getting on for double the return.

Happiness at work costs nothing. You can achieve a lot just by stopping some common business practices right away at a cost of zero.

For example, don't force your frontline staff to do stupid things like lie to customers.

Take away byzantine administrative processes and convoluted reporting systems.

Make sure the managers you appoint have great people skills.

Make sure your HR Department, if you have one, is less about policing transgressions and more about helping people to succeed.

Make sure you take some time every day to spend with people across your business. Find out how you can make their experience at work better tomorrow than it is today, and then action whatever they tell you.

None of that requires a major capital investment. None of that takes millions of pounds out your cashflow over the next five or ten years.

Yet you get the same productivity improvements normally associated with hugely expensive company-wide change programmes even though your investment has been little or nothing.

Happiness is a simple concept — hard to do sometimes, but simple to grasp.

What are you doing today to move you in the direction of 20-37% productivity improvements? Even if you don't get there straight away, anything you do will put money on your bottom line and cash in your bank account faster than almost anything else.

And all pretty much for free.

Time investment: Zero. This isn't about doing new things and adding to your workload. It's about using the time you already spend, just prioritising it a little differently.

Cash investment: Little or nothing. Along the way there might be the need to spend a little bit of cash to fix something that needs fixing, but most of the benefits can be delivered without spending a penny so you're in positive ROI territory pretty much from the start.

Strategy 97 – Don't tell, nudge

About 10 years ago a book called "Nudge" was at the top of the business bestsellers chart. Richard Thaler, one of the book's authors, won the Nobel Prize in Economics for his work on this aspect of behavioural economics.

But don't worry, we're not getting into economic theory here. We're just looking at how you can apply the principles to improve your business cash flow and keep more of what you earn in your own bank account by making your business operate more effectively.

You see, forcing people to do things they don't really want to do is expensive. One way or another.

It's either expensive now because people resent what they're being asked to do and deploy every stalling tactic in the book to avoid doing it. "Difficult conversations" with subordinates are a prime example of that, meaning your business misses out on the improvements it needs for longer than it should.

In the online world, forcing people to use a clumsy checkout process results in abandoned carts and lost sales for your business.

You'd have thought a process as critical as this for an online seller would have been perfected by now but coming across a positive shopping cart experience when buying online is a rare event for us all. Yet despite frequent customer complaints and sky-high data on cart abandonments, most businesses don't bother fixing them and so lose out on sales they could have made.

Forcing people to do things they don't want to do is expensive in the long run too. Customers drift away because it's too much like hard work to deal with your business. Your better people will do the same, meaning the ones who are left aren't as productive or insightful as they ones who've become disenchanted enough to find a job elsewhere.

Why "nudging" is important is that it allows you to move people in the direction you'd like them to go, but setting things up so they feel like it was their idea in the first place, so they do what you originally wanted, but without resentment or pushback.

Quick word of warning — there is no way to do this if what you're asking people to do is fundamentally unsound. No amount of nudging is going to get people to engage positively with broken systems or unsupportive managers.

But the concept can get you a long way.

Make it easier for people to do the right thing and they're more likely to do it without you putting time, effort and expense into making them do something they don't want to do.

One study in a school increased the amount of healthy food bought at lunchtimes by 18% just by rearranging lunch displays to give more prominence to healthy foods and less to unhealthy foods. It was a small change with a big effect that students were "nudged" into making.

So, what can you do in your business?

One place I worked had a historic problem with people turning up late for work put on a free breakfast each morning, but it was only available until half an hour before the normal start time. After that you had to pay the full price for your breakfast.

Did everyone take advantage of this? No. And some couldn't because of caring obligations of one sort or another.

But was on-time attendance dramatically improved with very little effort and almost no cost? Absolutely.

The canteen staff were in anyway so there was no increase in the labour cost. The ovens and grills were already on and the electricity was powering the lights anyway.

Yes, the business had to pay for some extra ingredients to make the breakfasts, but in most catering businesses the cost of ingredients is a relatively small part of the total price charged at the till. And in any event this business got an extra half-hour's productivity out of the people who came in early, so the breakfast service paid for itself pretty easily.

The alternative would have been lots of HR meetings, disciplinary procedures and more management and administration cost to police on-time attendance. And let's face it, a handful of extra people in HR would have cost a lot more over the course of the year than a few bacon sandwiches and cups of coffee did...while, with respect to my friends in HR, probably being somewhat less motivational.

Anything you can nudge your way to is almost certainly more effective and much less costly than policing your way towards the same goal. You get where you want to go faster when you work with people's motivation rather than against it.

Time investment: Little or nothing. Start with something small and work out a way to encourage the result you'd like to see, rather than enforcing it. Then work up from there.

Cash investment: Little or nothing — and anything you do spend is quickly returned by making faster progress towards your objectives or by achieving a better outcome than you would have done through compulsion alone.

Strategy 98 – Strength in diversity

It doesn't cost any more to hire a diverse group of people than a homogenous group, but the results from diverse groups of people tend to be better than from groups where everyone thinks and acts alike.

If you think about it, that's not necessarily a huge surprise. There's that old saying "if two people in my business think alike all the time then I don't need one of you".

Diversity can mean a range of different things. It might be making sure the proportion of women in senior roles mirrors their availability in the workforce. It might be having recruitment practices which encourage ethnic minority candidates to apply, knowing their views and beliefs will be respected within your business. It might just mean having a mix of people who think and experience life in a different way to yours and the other people working in the business.

I know some business leaders who think this all sounds like particularly hard work, something they don't have time for in their already-busy lives. But the truth is they don't have time not to do it.

The world has moved on from the 1960s when important people (by which I mean almost exclusively white, middle-aged men) sat in their offices and dictated memos giving orders about what people should do.

If that ever worked then...and I'm not sure it did, it's just there were no other options...it certainly doesn't work now.

And there are a range of diverse people trying to do what your business does in different ways in the hyper-competitive world of 21st Century commerce.

Whatever your business does, I can guarantee there's a programmer wearing jeans and a hoodie somewhere in Silicon Valley trying to work out how to turn your existing business model upside down and snaffle all the profits you make at present.

And there's also wealthy Middle Eastern sovereign wealth funds trying to work out if they could use their near-endless streams of cash to provide the capital to one of your competitors which will put you out of business.

And there's a business in China trying to work out how to do exactly what you do now, but at half the price you charge at the moment.

And that's just a small selection...truth is there are diverse groups of all sorts in every country of the world who are trying to get a bigger piece of the pie for themselves by undermining, in one way or the other, whatever your business model is now.

In time some of them will be successful, but you can prepare the ground now by having people who think differently and who represent different cultures around you. Unless you are a programmer yourself, it's unlikely you'll understand how they might work out a way to entice all your customers away. Ditto if you're not a Middle Eastern potentate or a Chinese industrialist.

And the truth is, even if you are one of those things, you can't be all of them.

Your best protection for the future is to build a business which is a fair spread of young and old, a mix of male and female, a range of different belief systems and a variety of ethnic backgrounds.

That's your best protection against future competitors and your best option for approaching your future in a more innovative and dynamic way.

However, improving diversity also makes good business sense now. McKinsey & Co research found that the more diverse a senior executive team was, the higher return on equity the business would earn. Top performing executive teams in terms of diversity earned a return on equity .7 times higher than those businesses in the bottom quartile for diversity.

So, if you're serious about wanting to maximise your profits, improving diversity is the way to go.

Time investment: Little or nothing. It takes no longer to hire a diverse group of staff than to hire candidates who are clones of the people you already have.

Cash investment: Nothing. It costs no more to hire a diverse group of people than a group of people who all think and act alike.

Strategy 99 – High margins don't necessarily mean high profits...and could mean the opposite

What would you rather have - a margin of 6.5% or a margin of 20%?

Seems obvious, right? But, perhaps surprisingly, you can be much better off investing in a business with 6.5% margins than a business with 20% margins.

WeWork — Wall Street's most monumentally embarrassing IPO attempt in recent years — boasted near-20% gross margin. Staid and traditional UK supermarket Tesco could only manage 6.5%.

Yet Tesco reported £4.2 billion in gross profits and £2.2 billion in net profit for their financial year to the end of February 2019.

While WeWork, in the year to 31 December 2018, made a gross profit of around $300m (around £250m) on revenues of £1.5 billion (approx. £1.25 billion), resulting in a pre-tax *loss* of $1.9 billion – more than the company's revenues for the year.

Margins on their own tell you very little, yet business owners often work hard to find ways of making that percentage margin as large as possible. Often, they would be better off putting their focus on the bottom-line performance and getting less excited about the percentage gross margin.

That's because margins can be artificially boosted by cutting costs to the point where the business struggles to deliver a decent service for the money they charge.

That makes the percentage margin look attractive, but often results in higher costs when the business needs to beef up their customer service teams to handle increased customer complaints, or incurs increased re-work costs in the factory when the goods supplied to customers aren't up to spec and need to be put right.

In a service industry, you can cut costs by running your business purely with people on minimum wage who are pretty confident they'd get another minimum wage job somewhere else if this one doesn't work out. In that environment, they're not necessarily highly motivated to serve customers as well as they might, leading to customers drifting away over time.

There's also a tendency to put cheaper, less qualified people on the job once the work has been won. I saw this particularly during my time in the advertising industry. A high-powered Account Director would be sent in to win the business by impressing clients with their skills, their stories and their presentation.

The next time the Account Director would be involved with the project would be an hour or so prior to the client pitch meeting when the junior account team who'd been working on the project while the Account Director was off pitching to other clients. The client thought they were getting the services of the Account Director who had impressed them so much. Usually they were getting the best results a team of juniors could come up with.

Sometimes the client noticed, but often they didn't, so it was an attractive economic model. For as long as it lasted, anyway.

Sooner or later the junior team would drop a catch because they just didn't know enough to do the job properly, the client would be livid, and the agency would (usually) be fired and get badmouthed to everyone the client knew.

How much more valuable would it be to have a long-term client than to try to pull a series of fast moves to artificially bump up profits, at least until the client noticed and went ballistic?

If you can find a way to make enough client pitches often enough, and don't care too much about your moral compass, you can make a pretty nice living like this. But this model is heavily dependent on being able to bring enough new clients through the front door at least as fast as disenchanted clients are leaving by the back door.

Not everyone can...and even if you can, it's a very expensive way to run a business. You need to spend a lot more money on marketing and promotion. Your sales team needs to be bigger. You end up paying out credits to clients for sub-standard work. Sooner or later your growth as a business will be hampered if its reputation for fast-talking and skulduggery precedes in in the marketplace.

At the heart of all this counterproductive behaviour is the disconnect between high margins and high profitability.

The most sustainable way to consistent profitability — the sort investors value the highest if you ever want to sell your business — is to save money on all the extra expenses you have keeping the show on the road when you play fast and loose with clients.

Save the extra costs of employing more salespeople, giving clients refunds and protecting your reputation with more investment in your business development and marketing.

What's more, since it costs the same to land a client either way, by running your business in ways that mean clients stay with you longer, you benefit from the compounding effects of having a flow of profits for much longer than if you burn through clients like fireworks on Bonfire Night.

Not only does that save you money in the short term. It builds your profits and cash flow in the long term too, keeping money in your own pocket instead of spending it to buy off unhappy clients, or find some new ones if that doesn't work.

Happy clients are what gets you long-term bottom-line profits. And while generally high margins are preferable to low margins, if you boost your margins by ripping off your customers, eventually they will notice and go elsewhere, depriving you of a stream of profits over many years which had been right there for the taking, if only you concentrated on the bottom line performance and not been too excited about artificially boosting your margins.

Time investment: None. It's actually easier to run your business without the high drama of clients blowing up when they've been let down by the product or service and taking their business elsewhere.

Cash investment: Zero. This is just about doing what you say you're going to do, doing it on time, and doing it to the quality you promised, or implied, to your client. And those are costs you've already covered through the prices you charge, so there's no additional cost to you.

Strategy 100 – Permission to speak, sir?

For those of you of a certain age, "Permission to speak, sir?" was one of the catchphrases from the classic BBC comedy "Dad's Army".

The very hierarchically minded corporal in the show always formally asked for permission from his commander before he said anything.

Many organisations are like that too. Nobody wants to speak up in case their intervention proves unwelcome and they're made to suffer in their next performance review.

This is one of the reasons large companies full of well-qualified people do an amazing number of catastrophically stupid things.

It's not that people don't realise the company's strategy is stupid, it's just there's is no mileage in speaking out. Much better to keep the salary coming through the door to pay the mortgage while they look for a different job in a company a little less stupid than where they work now.

In fairness to corporate leaders, even if you invite people to speak without fearing any repercussions, it's a brave subordinate who believes you. And it's really hard as a leader not to take offence when your pet project gets shot down in flames.

But there is a way to get at least some of this out, and it's an adaptation of something very clever Jeff Bezos does at Amazon.

Jeff Bezos makes sure there's an empty chair in every meeting to represent the customer and make sure their views are taken into account in every decision. I really like that idea because it allows people to put forward ideas from what they imagine the customer's reaction might be, instead of putting their own reputation on the line.

But I think that idea can be taken a step further.

What about having two empty chairs in each meeting, one to represent the customer and one to represent your staff? After all, unless you have those two groups completely on your side ultimately your business will go down one way or the other.

Frontline staff are often in the best position to enhance your firm's relationships with its customers because they talk to them every day. Motivate them well and they're your best salespeople. Demotivate them and you'll struggle to keep customers and get top prices for what you sell.

So, don't rely on someone having the courage to speak up in "Permission to speak, sir?" style. Encourage looking at anything your business does through the eyes of both the customers and your staff.

Whenever you find something that your customers and your staff think is a good idea, and your internal management team is satisfied the economics are good, you've hit pay-dirt. Odds are that's an idea which will become a big success and generate a constant stream of profits and cash flow into your business.

So make sure you've got two extra chairs in every meeting room — one for your staff and one for your customers. If one of your team poses a question through the lens of the staff or the customer, take it very seriously.

They're only saying what your staff, or your customers will be saying down the line anyway. What you're getting instead is a golden opportunity to improve the project or put it right in some way at little or no cost before you launch something in a cloud of hubris which falls on its face, costing you time, money and that all-important goodwill with customers and staff you need to run your business effectively.

Save money – buy two extra chairs for your meeting room and you'll make much better decisions for your business.

Time investment: If you don't already have a couple of extra chairs knocking around the business, five minutes online is all it takes to buy you an extra couple of meeting room chairs.

Cash investment: Somewhere between zero, if you already have some spare chairs, up to a few pounds if you don't. However, just one decision made better via the "two chair strategy" will more than pay back the cost of the furniture, so you get a high benefit for a low cost, something all businesses like to see.

Strategy 101 – What's the opposite?

In most businesses, people spend their time looking for evidence that things are on track and that their chosen path is a wise and sensible one.

That's understandable. They want to have a sense of professional pride in what they do, and they want you to value their input highly enough that you'll give them secure jobs and positive performance reviews.

I've sat in many board meetings and management meetings where the flimsiest of statistics are used to justify someone being on track for an improved performance this quarter compared to last quarter.

"We've had three positive letters from customers about our service" is a great thing to be reporting, especially if you're the person in charge of customer service.

But think about this.

If your business has 1000 customers and three of them write to you in positive terms this month, that's nice as far as it goes. And it's clearly better than having none.

What about the other 997 though – what did they feel about service this month?

At the very least, we know for sure they weren't sufficiently motivated by your organisation to want to write in about the service offered. That's a mathematical fact.

Some were probably actively dissatisfied with the service, the majority probably felt it was just a "meh" experience, not worthy of their time to express appreciation.

So rather than "we had two positive letters last quarter, and three this quarter, so we're on an upward trend", which is how these stats tend to get reported, it might be worth looking for evidence of the opposite.

What do we see through this lens? That 99.7% of your customer base had no reason to be enthusiastic about your service at all. Most of your customers probably couldn't care less. Some will be actively hostile.

Now, from where I'm sitting, that doesn't look remotely like a customer service success story.

And that's important to your cash flow because if something looks like it's doing OK, the tendency will be to leave that aspect of your business alone while you comb through other areas of the business which seem to have real problems to deal with, like last week's missed delivery, or the barrier on the car park which won't stay up to let cars in.

Do that for long enough and your customers will drift away because they just don't care enough about your business to hang around.

Never mind those other problems — a business without customers won't be around for long. Three positive letters from customers this quarter is more likely the sign of a major problem with your customer experience than an indication that everything is OK with customer service.

Most businesses just want to believe everything is OK with their customer service. So the directors get presented with some evidence which suggests that's the case, and the debate swiftly moves on.

Nobody looks at the opposite perspective, which might be a lot closer to the truth. By the time the positive letters have dried up and the hate mail starts pouring in, it's probably several months or years too late to do much about the problem.

That problem was there all along, but nobody looked at it because everything seemed to be OK.

Next time you're told "everything is fine – nothing to see over here" just take a few minutes and ask yourself what you would see if the opposite of what you're being told was true.

This isn't about deliberately mistrusting your team nor being excessively paranoid all the time, but when people have every incentive to tell you everything is OK, and to present evidence to back up what they're telling you, then it's natural that they'll be somewhat blinkered by that baggage.

If you want to get under the skin of what's really going on, take the opposite perspective and look for evidence that might be true instead. That way, you pick up problems at an early stage and can use your intervention to coach the members of your team to keep an eye on areas they might not have considered.

They almost certainly weren't trying to get you an objectively rational, independent view of their performance. They were only trying to find evidence which proved they were doing a good job, then presented that.

But don't be too harsh on your people – even captains of industry do that. Many an organisational collapse has had at its core the fact that nobody took the opposite point of view and went looking for evidence that might be the case.

You can be smarter than that and go looking where nobody else has. That way, you preserve your cash flow and protect your business for years to come. If you're serious about keeping your cash flow positive, that's a great place to start.

Time investment: Little or nothing. As you'll already be considering what you're being told and thinking about its implications, this is just a case of focusing your attention in a particular way, not in spending any more time.

Cash investment: Zero. This saves you getting sucked into complacency and allows you to make a head start on any issues the business might face long before your competitors will be addressing the same problems. That keeps the cash flowing into your bank account while your competitors run around in circles wondering what happened.

Cash Flow Mastery Programme

For full details of the three ways we deliver the Cash Flow Mastery programme, please visit us at CashFlowSurgeBook.com/Mastery

The Cash Flow Mastery programme is available as a 12-month executive coaching programme for you and your team, delivered on your premises.

There are very few slots available each year for the most prestigious version of our Cash Flow Mastery programme as it takes a significant investment in time to deliver the results we promise to clients. The charge for the Cash Flow Mastery programme delivered in this way is therefore commensurately significant, although it comes with a substantial guaranteed return on investment.

Acceptance onto the executive coaching programme is strictly by application and you'll need a turnover of at least £3 million (or $3million, or equivalent in local currency) to be accepted. Further details at CashFlowSurgeBook.com/Mastery.

The Cash Flow Mastery programme can also be delivered remotely via videoconference with six weekly 90-minute sessions on either an in-company or open programme basis.

This approach covers the same concepts and strategies as our executive coaching programme, but because you handle the follow-up and operationalisation of the process within your business, that reduces our involvement and we can pass the savings on to you.

That also means the Cash Flow Mastery programme makes more sense for businesses of all sizes, so there is no restriction on the size of business accepted onto the remote-delivered version of the programme.

In-company delivery gives us the opportunity to tailor parts of the programme to your own business needs and opportunities. The open programme clearly can't deliver that level of customisation but does bring the additional benefit of being able to compare notes with other business owners through the programme.

For both in-company and public programmes, there is a strict maximum of 10 participants in each group to ensure everyone gets the chance to participate fully.

Whichever option you choose, the programme content is the same across the six weekly sessions, the only difference is in the degree of customisation possible.

> **Whether you prefer our executive coaching programme, the in-company remote programme or the public programme, completing Cash Flow Mastery puts more money on your bottom line and more cash in your bank account, faster than you might think.**

If you're tired of worrying about cash flow...tired of crossing your fingers and hoping your customers pay on time like they're supposed to...tired of running your business hand-to-mouth...tired of not being paid until everybody else has been paid...tired of working ever-harder and seeing an ever-smaller return...then Cash Flow Mastery is for you.

> **You'll discover how to generate more profits and stronger cash flow by following a specific approach that maximises the amount of cash in your business.**

You'll also discover how to create and deliver on a distinctive mission that builds your sales income and allows you to charge higher prices for what you do...prices your customers will be glad to pay.

And you'll discover how to run your business at maximum efficiency and minimum cost, generating additional profits for your business and putting more cash into your bank account.

Whichever version of the Cash Flow Mastery programme you choose, the result is the same — more income generated at less cost means more profits and stronger cash flow.

Cash Flow Mastery delivers more cash to your bank account with less worry and less hassle. What's more, it frees up your time to pursue new opportunities and take your business forward, without worrying if the cash would be there to allow you to pursue your dreams.

That's what Cash Flow Mastery is all about – won't you join us?

Simply visit CashFlowSurgeBook.com/Mastery for all the details.

I look forward to meeting you there.

Alastair Thomson
Finance Director and Chief Financial Officer
CashFlowSurgeBook.com